TAWANA LOWERY

5 EASY STEPS
— TO —
LIFE CHANGING
PRAYER

Helping you Succeed with life's most Important Endeavor

5 Easy Steps to Life Changing Prayer

By Tawana Lowery

ISBN-13: 978-1512339024
ISBN-10: 1512339024

Design, Layout, and Typesetting by Alexander Becker
www.alexanderbecker.net

Book Cover design by: Rupa Ghosh
libzyyy@yahoo.com

Author Photo by Sandra Curtis Photography
sandracurtisphotography.com

CONTENTS

Dedication

I dedicate this book to my parents, Jerry and Frankie Lowery and to my dear sweet grandmothers. Thank you for all you did to instill a foundation of faith in my life.

Thank you

I want to thank my family for their support, encouragement and love. I also want to express my sincere gratitude to my wonderful friends in North Carolina. You have been a gift from God to me.

A special thank you to James Altucher for just being you and sharing it with the world.

INTRODUCTION

I hate trying to accomplish something important without enough information or the proper tools to make it happen. The pressure to succeed combined with a lack of what is needed feels like the perfect recipe for failure. Sometimes trying to pray or even thinking about prayer can provoke a similar response. The pressure to get it right combined with a lack of understanding on what to do, can seem like a mission impossible. Feelings of inadequacy, confusion or frustration can derail us before we even get started. If that describes some of your prayer experiences, then please don't feel alone. It's a struggle common to all flesh.

According to a 2012 Pew Research survey, more than 75 percent of Americans agreed that prayer is an important part of daily life. Surprisingly, that percentage has remained consistent over the past 25 years. Even among those who say they don't believe in God, 12 percent admit they pray, as reported in The Washington Post in June, 2013.

It seems a lot of us believe in the importance of prayer. The question is how many of us actually enjoy it? How many look forward to it? How often does prayer strengthen our relationship with God or make us feel more intimate with our Creator? More importantly, how often do we truly feel equipped for the task?

If the leaders of the flock are a reflection of the flock, then the answer may surprise you. According to an Ellis Research survey for Facts & Trends, less than 20 percent of church leaders say they are satisfied with their prayer lives. That means close to 80 percent are either completely or partially dissatisfied with prayer. That's an astounding figure, yet probably very representative of most people.

But what if I told you it doesn't have to be that way. What if you could understand with clarity exactly what to pray and how to pray it, regardless of the circumstance? What if you could recognize how God is presently speaking to you and what to do with it? What if you could learn to resolve hurts and conflicts in a way that transforms your thinking? What if prayer was enjoyable and easy to understand? What if you could experience God in the next 10 minutes?

The principles covered in this book will help you achieve all of that and more. I have devoted more than two decades to the study and practice of prayer. I have experienced and observed the uncertainty, fear and frustration that accompanies the activity of prayer. But I knew there had to be a better way. So I began to take notice of patterns and principles that produced consistent tangible results and exponentially improved my prayer experience. My goal for writing this book is to share those concepts and principles to help you succeed with the most important activity of your life, while dramatically improving your relationship with God.

5 Easy Steps to Life Changing Prayer offers easy to remember, practical tools to help you:

- End the cycle of uncertainty, intimidation and frustration that often describes most people's prayer experience.

- Improve your ability to hear God's voice and enjoy a stronger relationship with the person who loves you most.

- Understand what brings about transformational thinking and peace of mind.

- Pray in a manner that produces lasting healing for wounded emotions and relationships.

- Notice divine invitations for prayer you might be missing out on.

- Share what you've learned with others from a place of gratitude and respect.

Section One explains the 5 Step technique in a manner that anyone can understand and remember. Section Two provides several practical, in-the-trenches, real life examples on exactly how to apply each step. Included are numerous prayer examples you can easily adapt for your own situations. Section Three helps guide you on how to use the Scriptures in your daily prayer life.

This book will challenge your perception of prayer. It will change how you approach prayer and how you think about prayer. Once you begin to consistently apply these 5 Easy Steps, you will gain new insight on how God speaks through situations and provocations. And you'll grow in wisdom about how to pray for yourself and others with precision. I like to call them bull's eye prayers. Meaning, you won't have to wonder if you hit the mark.

5 Easy Steps to Life Changing Prayer will help you to quickly see and experience tangible results. You will be able

to rest with confidence that your prayers have been heard and engage the love and friendship of God for every detail of your life. So if you're ready for a brand new experience with prayer, if you're tired of the frustration, anxiety, uncertainty and confusion, then get ready to discover prayer the way it was meant to be; encouraging, engaging, enlightening. Get ready for life changing prayer.

SECTION ONE

THE 5 STEP TECHNIQUE

Step 1
THINK LOAVES AND FISHES

It might be helpful to think of prayer within the context of Jesus feeding the multitude. You can read all about it in Mark 6:30-44. Basically, the disciples were facing what they perceived to be an overwhelming complex problem. It was a situation they were ill prepared for. How is it possible for 12 fishermen in the middle of nowhere to feed five thousand people, plus all the women and children? They had no resources, no plan, no forewarning and no experience for the task. They were challenged to do something without the tools to succeed. Or so they thought.

"Send them home," was their first proposal. Their attitude was to simply walk away and put as much distance between themselves and the problem as possible. The last thing on their mind was to give the problem to Jesus. "What do you have," Jesus asked them. He wasn't the least bit concerned that the human resources match the need.

The disciples answered, "All *we* have are five loaves of bread and two fish." Actually it was more like a pack of crackers and a can of sardines. "Then bring it to me," Jesus said. Once they put their lack in the hands of Jesus, once they gave him the complexity of the situation, everything changed and they had more at the end than when they began.

This is the exact same attitude we should have about prayer. Jesus is not concerned with how much we know or how eloquently we can verbalize our issues. He's not waiting to see how fast we figure things or how well we can package a polished conclusion. God wants us to go to him and say, "All I have is a pack of crackers and a can of sardines. But I'm giving it to you in faith, believing that you'll take it and produce from it more than I need."

In other words, if we are willing to just pray about the little bit we know or don't know to pray about, it can and will produce more than we could ever imagine. Regardless of how clueless and inadequate we feel in the process, even if we have no idea what to say, Step One is always the best place to start. We need to Think Loaves and Fishes by putting our inadequacy in the hands of a miracle working Savior.

For years I thought I needed to have a general idea about a solution or at least a rough draft before I could go to God in prayer. Otherwise why would he listen? That mind set created a stumbling block in my heart and prevented me from experiencing the very thing I was in need of. I had no idea I could go to God and simply say, "Lord, I'm clueless."

Once I realized that God was okay with my cluelessness, it transformed my prayer life. It liberated my heart and mind from the prerequisite of trying to figure something out before I could take it to God in prayer. Now, if a person or situation provokes me and I can't easily decipher why, I

Think Loaves and Fishes. No matter what it feels like, no matter how confusing or upsetting the event, regardless of how clueless I might feel, my first prayer is a Loaves and Fishes prayer. I take the little bit I have and put it in the hands of Jesus and say:

> *Lord I'm clueless. I don't know what to pray. I don't even know where to start or what to say. But I bring my cluelessness to the cross and ask that you would replace it with wisdom, insight and understanding. Speak to my heart and show me what to pray next. Amen.*

Often times our resistance to prayer comes from a lack of experience with God's strength to help us. All we know is our own weakness or the collective weakness of those around us. It's like coming to the end of the road at the precipice of the Grand Canyon. But it is only the end of the road for our flesh. It is the beginning of the road for God's power to create something miraculous in us and for us.

The Bible instructs us that "in our weakness, his power is made perfect." That means it's okay to feel inadequate or clueless when you pray. In fact, this scripture gives us permission to be weak. What we need when we engage God is usually the opposite of what the world, and even religion tells us. With God, weakness is the key to strength and cluelessness is the key to wisdom.

Maybe you feel the way I used to feel. Maybe you find it difficult to pray because you don't know where to start. Maybe you believe you need at least half the equation figured out before you begin. Rather than letting those thoughts become a stumbling block, use them as a stepping stone. Use the cluelessness and weakness as an invitation to press in towards God's loving hands and open arms. Think of it as a toddler who's just beginning to walk. Then take every step to God in prayer and ask Him for the ability to take the next one, and the next and the next. Give him every tiny fish and every little crumb. You can start right now by simply praying:

> *Heavenly Father, just thinking about prayer makes me confused and frustrated. The confusion and frustration tempts me to give up before I even get started. The truth is I don't know where to begin, what to say or if my prayers will even make a difference. But I give you my limited understanding along with my all the doubt and lack of experience. In return, I asked for new revelation concerning your thoughts about prayer and how much you have made yourself available to help me. Lord, forgive me for putting faith in my own limitations instead of faith in your unlimited resources. Remove the blocks that prevent me from hearing your voice. I give you permission to reveal what I need to know so I can know you better. Amen."*

See how easy that was! ☺ That was a Loaves and Fishes prayer. Come to think of it, everything we present to God is loaves and fishes. He's the one that makes something useful and beneficial of it. Our resources and efforts are never enough, and never will be enough. But it's okay. That's why God sent us a Savior. The world may not give you permission to have limitations, but the world did not create you and it will never sacrifice itself to save you.

Something else to consider is that God wants a relationship with us more than we want one with him? This is an important truth to remember because prayer is, at its core, the primary method by which we stay connected to God. Prayer was God's idea. It was his design for enabling us to know and experience him for the purpose of redemption, restoration and relationship. Therefore, any effort we make to connect with our Heavenly Father is always welcomed.

But you may be thinking, "What if it has been a long time since I last prayed? Will God still listen to me? Does he still care?" In a word…YES! God is not keeping score on us and he's not holding a grudge. Sometimes we picture God as this grumpy relative who responds to our phone calls with condemnation or accusations like, "I thought you were dead. You haven't called me in 6 months. Do you need money or something?" My personal favorite is… the silent treatment.

God is not like that. He's doesn't get-off by putting us on guilt trips. He's not seated on his throne, arms crossed, tapping his foot and saying, "Well it's about time you showed up. Don't think you can just waltz in here after being away so long and expect anything from me!" That's who we are. It's not who God is.

Instead imagine you have just arrived home from a lengthy military operation. How would your best friend greet you? How would your dog greet you? I want you to see God as someone longing to give you a gigantic hug on every possible occasion. Each time you think about praying, visualize God smiling at you, anxious to wrap his arms around your neck with love and compassion. Prayer is your opportunity for a heavenly hug!

The key take-away from Step One is that little is much when God is in it. If a mustard seed is all you have, then plant it. Sometimes the issues plaguing our heart can feel like boulders or an un-scalable mountain. But taking down the mountain starts with a grain of sand. Removing the sand loosens the pebbles, then the pebbles loosen the rocks, the rocks dislodge the boulders and the boulders bring down the mountain. In other words, your most powerful prayer might be found in three little words, "God, I'm clueless."

Step One Prayer

"Heavenly Father, forgive me for thinking I have to figure it all out before I can call on you. The truth is, I am clueless, more than I want to admit. But it is for this very reason that you sent me a Savior. Jesus took my cluelessness so I could receive the clues I need to walk with you in this life. Enable me to trust you with each step along the way. Give me greater revelation of just how much you are for me and not against me. Take my heart, change my heart, encourage my heart and speak to my heart by the power of your Spirit. Amen."

Personal Reflection

1. Think about a situation or relationship that has been difficult to pray about. Maybe it is something that overwhelms you each time it comes up.

2. Take each item on your list to God in prayer as if you were handing him a basket of tiny fish. Pray one or two of the prayers listed above inserting your issue or relationship as the topic to pray about.

3. After you have prayed about it, be sensitive to thoughts or ideas that may come to your mind or emotions.

4. Write down those new thoughts, ideas or revelations and use them as an opportunity for more Loaves and Fishes prayers.

_____

_____

_____

_____

_____

_____

_____

_____

_____

_____

_____

_____

_____

Step 2
BE HONEST

Honesty is a foundational tenant in all healthy thriving relationships. Without honesty, we don't know what to believe, where we stand with each other, what to expect, how to plan, how to invest (time and money), how to converse, or how to operate in the normal day-to-day comings and goings. Think about it. Without a foundation of truth, what foundation is there to build anything on?

If prayer involves engaging God in a relational manner, then honesty with him is just as foundational as any other relationship we value. I have learned that the best relationships are those with whom I can be the most honest, without fear of judgment, rejection or retaliation. That's exactly the type of relationship God wants us to have with him. In fact, Psalm 145:18 tells us, "The Lord is near to all who call on him, to all who call on him in truth."

Many people feel anxiety about being totally honest with God. And it's probably for the same reason they have anxiety about being honest with people. Although our reason for not trusting people may be valid, we have to be mindful of projecting those experiences on to our relationship with God. He is not a man that he should be judged as a man or mankind. In fact, God is not like anyone we have ever known or ever will know. Meditating on this will help us recognize the numerous false judgments we make concerning God's trustworthiness.

Some reason we don't trust God might include the following.

We don't know him: It takes time to know someone's habits, their personality and how they manage their life. Part of relationship development includes evaluating whether or not the person can be trusted. If God is a stranger, then the question you need to ask yourself is, "Why?" I can pretty much bet it's not because he wants it that way.

Our experience with people: This can includes violations of trust or someone not meeting our standards of trust. Once a trust or expectation is broken, especially if it happens numerous times with numerous people, it tempts us to harden our hearts or become cynical and guarded with almost everyone. Including God.

What we have been taught: Phrases we use a lot include, "trust but verify," "never tell anyone what you truly think," "never share anything you don't want repeated." All those suggestion sound like reasonable common sense ideas. And in a world full of people trying to save their own butt, it's a reality we have to embrace. However, do you think it's in our best interest to have that same mindset with God? After all, whose butt is God trying to save? His or yours?

What we inherited from the Garden of Eden: Some find it hard to be honest with God because they feel a sense of guilt and shame. They don't understand the depths of God's love to cover their wrong doings. Our lack of understanding creates fear and the fear creates separation. That is the same response Adam and Eve had after The Fall. They ran away and hid themselves because of fear and uncertainty. But who pursued who? Who covered who? Who moved heaven and earth to restore the relationship?

Fear of Rejection: In his book "The Power of No," James Altucher describes a season in his life when he falsified the truth about his true self for fear of being rejected. He was afraid his true self would not be acceptable to others. All of us have felt these same pressures and temptations.

In my own life, my most redemptive experiences happened as a result of being gut honest with God about how I felt or what I thought regarding people, life or situations. For example, a few years ago, my mother called to invite me to spend Sunday afternoon with her. The agenda included attending her church and going to lunch. Neither of which I wanted to do. How's that for honesty? But, since it was my mother, I reluctantly agreed.

As the day of our visit drew closer the anxiety increased. By the time Saturday evening rolled around, I was a nervous wreck! It was a routine I had become all too familiar with. However, on this occasion I decided to talk to God about it. The conversation went something like this:

Me: God, I am soooo dreading spending the day with my mother.

God: Why?

Me: Because of the way she makes me feel.

God: Okay. How does she make you feel?

Me: Like I'm not good enough, like I never measure up to her expectations.

God: So, why does it bother you so much?

Me: … (a deep breath with a deep sigh)…

God: How would it make you feel if you could meet her expectations? What would you gain by gaining her acceptance?

Me: I think (long pause)… I think it would give me peace.

God: It would give you peace in your heart?

Me: Yes, it would. It really would.

God: Maybe… rest in your soul?

Me: Yep, that too.

God: Hmmm. That's a lot of pressure.

Me: Tell me about it.

God: What if you could have peace… whether she accepts you or not?

Me: Are you kidding me? That would be awesome.

God: What if you could enjoy rest in your soul even if you never measured up to a single one of her expectations?

Me: Is that actually possible?

God: If peace and rest came from meeting her expectations or gaining her acceptance, then… why would you need me?

Me: Good grief! I never thought about it like that.

God: Well, maybe it's time to start.

Me: Wow God! You are sooooo right. And I am soooo sorry.

God: If peace and rest is what you want, you can have it as a free gift. Then you can stop freaking out about your mother's demands.

24

```
Me:     ...

God:    All you have to do is ask me. Want to pray
        about it?

Me:     Absolutely!
```

Obviously I prayed about the issue. I asked God to forgive me for seeking peace and rest from my mother's acceptance rather than receiving it from him as a free gift, regardless of whether she approved of me. I also forgave my Mom for doing to me what was done to her. Being honest with God about what was in my heart not only delivered me from pain, but also gave me insight on how to forgive and cover generations of hurt.

I guess you're wondering how the visit with my mom turned out. Truthfully, I did not enjoy attending her church. Some churches just give me a colossal headache. But lunch with my mother was surprisingly delightful. As a result of being honest with God, he freed my heart of anxiety. That allowed me to feel secure and at peace in his acceptance of me. Time with my mom was filled with easy cheerful girl talk about past vacations and places we would like to visit someday.

About half way through the conversation she paused and made a comment I never expected to hear. "I need to ask your forgiveness," she said. "Forgiveness for what," I replied. Glancing down at her coffee cup she answered, "I've put a lot of demands on you – demands I couldn't live up to myself. I'm sorry for doing that." "It's okay mother," I assured her with a smile. "I've already forgiven you. And besides, if you could have met the needs of a daughter's heart, I would have never known how much I needed a Savior. The pain was the vehicle that drove me to the cross. So, it all worked out for good!"

You see, honesty with God is not for his benefit. It's for ours. We've somehow determined that there is nothing but downside if we are honest with God about our thoughts, our feelings and our unbelief. The truth is, there's nothing but downside if we're not.

Nothing we can say will shock him or make him upset with us. No need to worry about God rejecting us once our true self is known. He already knows us. He created us. He formed us. And he loved us enough to send his only son to die for us. The more honest we are, the more God is endeared towards us. The more his heart is moved with compassion towards us. As the Psalmist said, "the Lord is near to those who call upon him, to those who call upon him in truth." If you find it difficult to be honest with God, then pray this prayer. Let his love begin to heal you from all the experiences that have prejudiced your heart towards his trustworthiness and care for you.

Step Two Prayer

Heavenly Father, I've been reluctant to talk with you honestly about what's in my heart. I've been hesitant to express how I truly feel and what I truly think about people, circumstances and even my own life. I've allowed my experience with others to prejudice my heart towards you. I've judged my experience with you will be the same as all my earthly experiences. Father, forgive me.

Give me a new frame of reference concerning the benefits of an honest relationship with a loving Father. Help me to see the upside of being truthful with you. And give me wisdom about how to share this understanding with others. Amen.

Personal Reflection

1. How does the idea of honesty with God make you feel?

2. Think of experiences where trust was violated with people. What judgments did you make about relationship from those experiences?

3. What are your thoughts about being transparent with people. Do you feel safe being transparent with God? If not why not?

4. Once you have identified these area that might be blocking your ability to be honest with God, return to the previous prayer and customize it to include the new revelations you have discovered.

_____

_____

_____

_____

_____

_____

_____

_____

_____

_____

_____

_____

Step 3
ASK A DIVINE QUESTION

A few years ago, park service officials in Washington, D.C. noticed an unusual amount of wear and tear on one of the monuments. After further investigation, they discovered it was due to excessive scrubbing to clean off the bird droppings. They began experimenting with different cleaning methods in hopes of reducing the impact. But nothing helped. So they installed nets to keep the birds out, but the tourist complained.

Finally they asked the question, "Why do we have so many birds coming to this particular monument?" After conducting a few studies it was determined that the birds were coming to eat insects. So park service workers experimented with different insecticides. But each one only worked for a short period of time. And soon the original problem returned.

Their frustration with the situation and the lack of a solution prompted another question, "Why do we have so many insects swarming the monument?" Turns out, the bright lights illuminating the memorial in the evenings were drawing the insects. They discovered by simply turning on the lights one hour later each night, they were able to eliminate more than ninety percent of the insects.

Reducing the amount of insects reduced the bird droppings, which reduced the scrubbing and the wear and tear on the memorial. The brushes, netting, and insecticides simply addressed the symptoms. The root cause was the lighting. Once that was addressed, the problem went away.

So what on earth do bird droppings on a monument have in common with prayer? For a lot of us, praying is mostly focused on solving a problem from situations or difficulties we can't overcome. Often, what we have concluded the problem to be is nothing more than a symptom of a greater issue. Because we think we know what the problem is, we think we know what a solution should look like.

But, problem-solving prayers lock us in to one-dimensional, linear thinking. We limit our dialogue with God with a fix-it mentality controlled by humanistic cause and effect reasoning and experiential bias. Problem solving prayers focus on symptoms without addressing root causes.

In case you're wondering what this looks like from a heavenly perspective, go to YouTube and search on "dogs chasing their tail." Is it any wonder why so many people become weary and frustrated with prayer? At some point we all get tired of running in circles.

May I propose a different approach? What if you started asking Divine Questions? What if, instead of focusing on the symptoms, you began asking God questions that point to the root cause? Asking a Divine Question opens us up to receive Divine Solutions. It elevates our perspective and allows us to think about people and situations the way God does. Divine Questions sound like this:

Why is this person or situation stealing my peace?

We covered an example of this in Step 2. This is where being gut honest pays big dividends. We get tripped up on demanding the person or situation change. Asking this divine question shifts the focus to why it bothers YOU? If something is stealing your peace, maybe it's because your peace is in something that can be stolen. Find out what conditions you've placed on having peace and you'll get to the root cause of why it's being stolen. Hint: There is only one giver of peace. Peace is a person not a condition.

What am I putting my faith or hope in other than God?

Some answers might include: a job, a credit score, a missed opportunity, a past mistake, another person's decisions, your own ability or inability.

Answering this question will help you locate where you've misplaced your faith. By the way, misplaced faith is where most disappointment and false standards originate.

Why can't I love this person the way God does?

It's just so much easier to write someone off or marginalize them instead of praying about why you can't love them. Not that they haven't given you plenty of reasons to feel that way.

Pondering this question will help you think about what you are hoping to get from the relationship. After you answer that question, then think about what it would give you if you received what you're hoping for. Next, ask yourself if you were ever supposed to get those things from another person (who is also looking for the same thing from another person). Maybe everyone is just looking for love in all the wrong places. That might explain a 50 percent divorce rate. I'm just saying.

The excuses I typically make for not loving someone include: Because it means they get away with it or because they're a pain in the butt. But mostly it's because I don't know God's love for me greater than the other person's decisions or behavior.

Who have I judged will bear the cost?

Ouch and double ouch! I'll bet you've never asked yourself this question before. At least not out loud. But I'll bet you thought about it. And I'll bet your conclusion was that YOU would have to bear the cost. Where did that conclusion come from? Have you thought about that?

Answering this question helps reveal our unbelief in God's desire and ability to be there for us. It's easy to imagine his help and provision for others. You're going to love the chapter on Burdens. Trust me on this one.

Am I trying to get a handle on the future or a handle on knowing God as my future?

This question will help reveal what is controlling the motives of our heart. It will also expose what we put our trust in.

For example, if we judge (although subconsciously) that having a better handle on the future will give us a sense of security, then what we would actually experience is never having it. If we are constantly in need of something we don't have, then our soul will never find rest? The future is always in the future. Think about it.

Am I seeking fairness from the world or favor from God?

Contemplating this question helps reveal where we believe blessing and restoration come from. It is also a reflection of what we truly value and what we put our hope in.

Fairness isn't favor. And favor isn't fair. But if we don't have a frame of reference for favor, if we've never been favor's recipient, then fairness is all we can hope for. It's our only consolation prize.

The main take away from Step 3 is that problem solving prayers don't solve too many problems because they are mostly focused on symptoms. Even though God's love and grace is available to us where we are, I believe he wants to elevate our thinking with Divine Questions. Then we can more easily spend our time and energies on root causes and watch the symptoms take care of themselves.

You may be thinking, "What if I can't come up with a Divine Question?" Then start with Step 1 and Step 2. In other words offer to God your empty hands and honestly confess that you don't know how to do it. You could simply pray:

Step Three Prayer

"Heavenly Father, I don't know how to ask a Divine Question. All I have are problem solving prayers and I'm clueless how to pray any differently. But I commit my clueless understanding to you and ask that you would replace it with inspiration from your heart to mine. I also bring my unbelief that you will actually give me what I need. Forgive me for my doubting heart and create in me the capacity for faith in you. Teach me how to ask a Divine Question, by the power of your Spirit at work in me. Amen."

Personal Reflection

1. Reflect on problems you are trying to solve with problem solving prayers?

2. List the results of those prayers? Have the problems been solved?

3. Try applying the Divine Questions listed above to your particular situation.

4. Ask God for revelation on what other Divine Questions need to be asked.

_____

_____

_____

_____

_____

_____

_____

_____

_____

_____

_____

_____

_____

_____

_____

Step 4
TAKE AN EYE EXAM

We often use the phrase "it takes one to know one." What that basically means is our ability to notice a particular fault or weakness in others comes from the familiarity of it within ourselves. If we are troubled or bothered about a behavior or character issue in another, it is because we are subconsciously troubled or bothered by it in ourselves. That kind of insight can be a blessing, depending on what you do with. It is especially true with regards to prayer.

There is a passage in Matthew 7:2-5, where Jesus is mentoring his disciples on this topic. He asked, "Why do you see the splinter that is in your brother's eye, but do not notice the plank that is in your own eye? Or how can you say to your brother, 'Let me take the splinter out of your eye,' when there is the plank in your own eye? First take the plank out of your own eye, and then you will see clearly to take the splinter out of your brother's eye.

Have you ever noticed how this passage is mostly used to judge people who are judging other people. How we think anything good can come from that cycle of condemnation is beyond me. See what I mean? Even that statement is judgmental. Which leads to my next point; we all judge each other, everybody, all the time, since the beginning of time. It's part of our human existence just like breathing.

As humans we will never stop noticing what we perceive to be the shortcomings or character flaws in others. Since God understands this part of our humanity, he gave us some heavenly instructions on how to approach it when it happens. If you examine the passage a little closer you'll notice that Jesus never said it wouldn't happen. What he said was, do something else when it does happen. And that something else is to Take an Eye Exam, a spiritual eye exam.

Each time I visit my optometrist, she examines my eyes in order to tell me what adjustments are needed to improve my vision. She writes a prescription to strengthen my weaknesses and correct any distortions. Without the exam I wouldn't know what to adjust. Without applying the necessary adjustments, I would have a very difficult time managing through life.

There are a lot of things I can't do without contacts or glasses. Reading small print, threading a needle, driving at night in the rain, and working on the computer are just a few examples. Can you imagine what would happen if, instead of wearing my contact or glasses, I simply demanded that the world around me adjust to my visual limitation? That would be completely nonsensical. And yet, that is exactly what we do, in a spiritual sense.

If we refuse to take a spiritual eye exam, then we live with a distorted reality. And rather than seeing things through a spiritual lens, we often demand the world around us (especially people) adjust to our limited vision. We say things like, "I'm only telling you this for your good?" But if we don't take an eye exam first to understand God's heart about the situation, how can we truly know what is best for the other person. Only God knows that. Without his perspective, we're reduced to operate from our perspective.

As a practical example of how to apply this to the subject of prayer, let's use a couple of easy targets; Preachers and Politicians. (Apologies if you're either. God help you if you're both.) On occasion, God will prompt me to attend a church that I am not familiar with in order to pray for the congregation or the leadership.

One particular Sunday I attended a megachurch in my community. When the minister began to speak, I immediately noticed some nuances about his demeanor that really jumped out at me. So I wrote down what I saw and felt. Keep in mind it had nothing to do with what he was saying. It had everything to do with what he was not saying and the way he was not saying it.

This is what I wrote: "The pastor sounds like he is burdened and bothered that everything is up to him. He seems frustrated with the congregation. There is a sense of urgency, fear and desperation in his voice. He seems like he is under a lot of pressure to impress, perform or make an impact. I think he's afraid of failing."

At that moment I had to make a decision. I could judge him and chalk it up to one more unpleasant religious experience. Or I could see it as spiritual insight on how to pray for the pastor. As I looked at what I wrote I knew I had to own it. In other words I had to realize that my ability to notice all those issues in him was due to the familiarity of it in my own life. I chose to Take and Eye Exam. Here is what I prayed.

> *Heavenly Father, The fact that I can see all these issues in this minster is because I have struggled*

with the same things in my own life. Maybe they were created from a different set of circumstances, but it produced the same response. It bore the same fruit.

Lord, just like this man, I too have had moments when I felt everything was up to me. I know what it's like to feel dumped on, unappreciated, misunderstood and afraid to fail. What I wanted most in those situations was to know that someone cared about me, that someone had my back, that someone loved me whether I could perform or not. The reason I felt so burdened was because I didn't know you as my source of help, companionship and acceptance.

Father, if that is what controls this pastor, I ask that you would forgive him for thinking everything is up to him. Forgive us both for not calling on you. Forgive us for taking on a mantel of responsibility that only you can carry. Forgive him for his unbelief is your all sustaining grace and love purposefully directed towards him. Give this pastor whatever measure of grace he needs to cast all his care on you as he grows in the knowledge of how much you care for him. Amen.

This is just one example of how to take an eye exam. But you could easily apply the same technique with most any person or situation. When God allows us see the situation from his perspective it turns our hearts from judgment to love. So the next time you notice a short coming in someone else such as selfishness, stubbornness, shortsightedness, deceit, fear, anger, and so on, stop for a moment and Take an Eye Exam.

First ask yourself if you have ever struggled with or experienced the same issue. Although your particular circumstances may have been different the temptations of the heart are common to all flesh. Man looks on the outward appearance, but God is concerned with our heart.

It doesn't mean the other person gets a pass. It doesn't mean you have to accept the behavior. It simply means you get to see the issues of their heart with a heavenly lens. It means you care enough about how much God cares about them (and you) to gain a spiritual perspective.

Just for fun, pick your least favorite politician to practice on. Don't think about how to change them or whether you agree with their ideology. It's not about right or wrong. It's about receiving Gods heart and mind for them and you. It's about laying our life down for someone else, for their deliverance and ours.

First, list the negative traits or issues you see in the person you have selected. Your list might include things like arrogance, stubbornness and entitlement. But it might also include fear, desperation, panic, blame shifting and so on.

Now for the courageous part; Take each one of those negative traits and sincerely ask yourself if you have ever acted the same way or displayed the same behavior. I'm sure you will find at least two or three common struggles.

Next, ask God to show you why you behaved the same way. What was controlling your heart? What were you putting your faith in other than God? What did you believe you could be or have if you actually achieved what you were trying to achieve? Most likely it was a sense of well being, security, peace, hope for the future or rest for your soul.

Finally, ask God to forgive both of you for trying to find life, peace, hope and rest from something or someone other than Christ. Ask God to deliver both of you to a place of faith in him and his grace and love. Then take note if your thoughts or feelings change towards this person going forward. Notice if your heart changes from judging them to loving them. Okay, maybe love is too much to ask. It is a politician after all. ☺ So let's just go for understanding.

And remember, it's the love of God not the judgment of man that brings someone to repentance. So ask yourself if you truly care about their soul or if you are only concerned with how their behavior might affect your life? Well guess what? Self preservation might be the very thing that controls them. See what I mean? Having fun yet?

Step Four Prayer

Heavenly Father, I think what you're asking me to do is to be willing to lay my life down for others the way you have done for me (and the whole world). Lord, if that's the case, then give me a new revelation about the blessings attached to it.

Thank you for giving me new insight on how to pray for others and how to experience your love for me as a result. I give you permission to unravel this in my heart and mind according to my frame and character. Speak Lord. Your servant is listening. Amen.

Personal Reflection

1. Think about at least 2 people in your daily routine that cause you to be unsettled or irritated.

2. Use the steps described with the Politician example to Take an Eye Exam for each of those individuals.

_____

_____

_____

_____

_____

_____

_____

_____

_____

_____

_____

_____

_____

_____

_____

_____

_____

_____

Step 5
BE PROACTIVE

Researchers at the American Psychological Association conducted a study on the impact of proactive attitudes among college graduates. The study revealed that students who rated high in proactive personality were more likely to secure a job soon after graduation. This was contributed in part to their belief that they could actively influence their environment and circumstances through personal actions.

Other studies have shown that proactive parents are more engaged in their children's lives and are intentional about fostering their child's development. Proactive couples are deliberate about maintaining good communication. They purposefully plan time together for intimacy and fun. And employees who rank high in proactive personality are promoted more often and earn higher salaries.

The attitudes of proactive behavior also include showing initiative and taking action in order to effect meaningful change, using foresight by thinking and acting ahead of anticipated events and noticing patterns or shifts as a signal to make an adjustment. University of Alabama head football coach Nick Saban believes anticipation and preparation are useful tools whether on or off the field. (The 2013 Iron Bowl notwithstanding. Roll Tide anyway!)

It seems every area of life can benefit from the habits and behaviors of a proactive attitude. This is especially relevant as it relates to our prayer life. Unfortunately prayer is frequently considered a means of last resort. It's something many turn to after everything else has failed.

Can you imagine having a "last resort" attitude regarding parenting, maintaining a car or planning your career? That would be an irresponsible immature way to live. And yet too often people turn to prayer from a reactive posture instead of a proactive one.

Maybe you're wondering what being proactive in prayer means. First it means considering prayer as a lifestyle, as the first resort and not the last. It means taking time each day to call on a Savior for guidance and help. It means intentionally putting God in the driver's seat of life so life doesn't drive us crazy.

I do a lot of praying in my car or when I'm exercising. Sometimes I simply ask my Heavenly Father to guide my steps, to give me wisdom and good judgment no matter what or who I encounter. I ask for grace to go before me and mercy to follow after me. Basically, I commit my day and my way to God. Proverbs 3 explains that if we trust in the Lord and commit our way to him, he will make our paths straight.

There are so many unknowns in life. But there is someone who knows everything from beginning to end. He knows the thoughts and intents of every heart. It just makes good sense to call on someone like that for help, early and often. One way to do this is to start your day by praying:

"Lord, I ask that you direct my steps and my desires today. Bring my will in alignment with yours. I give you my agenda and ask that you would bless it or redirect it as you see fit. Give me wisdom to see your hand and a greater sensitivity to hear your voice in all my comings and goings. Thank you for loving me and caring about the details of my life. Give me the ability to find my peace in knowing you regardless of what the day may bring. Amen."

Secondly, being proactive includes regular, frequent Scripture reading. According to world renowned evangelist, Dr. Billy Graham, reading the Holy Scriptures gives opportunity for God's Spirit to speak directly to us through his Word. As a result, our hearts are stirred to pray. It's a simple way to proactively make deliberate consistent scripture deposits in our heart and mind.

Life works overtime to make us discouraged and upset. Filling our minds with the truth of God's Word produces a fat Scripture bank account to help us overcome those inevitable rainy days. Section 3 of this book contains some ideas to help you. I included my own scripture favs along with a proven method for applying them to your prayer life.

Lastly, Proactive Prayer means becoming an active participant in our own sanctification. In Christianity, sanctification refers to the process of being set apart by God for a special purpose. It begins at salvation and continues throughout our entire lifetime. Our participation is not in an effort to sanctify ourselves through our own works. But it does involve a willing cooperation with God's desire to renew and restore our hearts and minds; to make us more like Christ and less like everyone else.

One of the primary ways we can participate in this process is to adopt the habit of asking God to reveal our blind spots. Most automobiles have a blind spot that impairs the driver's vision at certain angles. A lot of collisions happen because a hazard is hidden from view. In a similar way, people have spiritual blind spots that inhibit the ability to see potential hazards to our soul.

More specifically, spiritual blind spots are those hidden things that distort our understanding of God or create static in our relationship with him. They are typically formed through the false ideas and beliefs we adopt as truth based on our experiences with society, family or religion.

When my son was young he was given a VCR copy of the movie Batman, starring Jack Nicholson as The Joker. The giver's motives were thoughtful and well intentioned. I'm sure they believed they were giving my son something useful. What he received, however, was a copy of a copy of a copy of another copy.

The resolution was grainy and fuzzy making it difficult to distinguish details or see the characters clearly. To make matters worse, the audio and video were slightly out of synch. Nevertheless, it was the Batman movie. The characters the script and the music were all present. But the entire movie was misrepresented because of how far removed it was from the original.

Given with sincerity? Absolutely! Presented in its original format? Absolutely not! Was the giver ignorant or even neglectful concerning what they presented? Of course they were. Most likely they simply copied a copy that was given to them.

In a similar manner, this is how many people have formed their ideas and opinions about God and life. They've been given copies of copies of copies, thousands and thousands of times removed from the original source. Most of those copies were given with sincerity and some were given in ignorance. Not knowing any better, they were accepted with sincerity or ignorance.

At some point we all find ourselves on the receiving end of the unredeemed distorted ideas passed to us from family, society, friends or religion. Some were given to us in ignorance and others with sincerity. Some came to us generationally and some we adopted ourselves based on our own distorted ideas. It's a process that's been going on since the Fall of Adam and Eve. The lyrics from a Bastille song entitled "Flaws" says it perfectly.

All of your flaws and all of my flaws

They lie there hand in hand

Ones we've inherited, ones that we learned

They pass from man to man

But regardless of the particulars or the delivery method by which the fallacies were presented, a proactive disciple takes responsibility to seek God for revelation on the spiritual blind spots those ideas created. The good news is, our Savior stands totally ready and willing to help us.

An example of someone who understood the impact of spiritual blind spots is found in Psalm 139:23-24. David proactively employed God in prayer and wrote him a blank check, so to speak. He asked God to search him and show him anything and everything that needed to be changed. He didn't go in fear or with a sense of condemnation. He already knew God's love.

But in order to improve the relationship, David asked God to show him the spiritual blind spots that might be standing in the way. David called on God's divine intervention to expose the distortions and static preventing him from becoming all God had in mind for him. I think this is one of the reason God described David as "A man after his own heart." David was determined to cooperate with God in his own sanctification.

The Bible instructs us in 1John 1:8-9 that "If we say we have no sin the truth is not in us. But if we confess our sins, He (God) is faithful and just to forgive us our sins and cleanse us from all unrighteousness." Put another way, when we live as if we have no spiritual blind spots, then we are walking in denial and setting ourselves up for a collision. But if we ask God to reveal our blind spots, he is loving and kind and will tenderly reveal the hidden things we might be missing in order to transform and renew us.

Giving God permission to reveal our blind spots is a proactive way of asking him to show us what we don't know that we need to know. It means we desire to cooperate with his spirit to remove anything that might be standing in the way of becoming the people we don't know we can become; the person God has predestined us to become.

While on this proactive prayer journey, it's also important to remember that Jesus is the origin of proactive behavior. The Bible says in Hebrew 7:25 that Jesus is ALWAYS interceding on our behalf before the Father. That means he is proactively praying for us continually. In fact, that is what he lives for. Jesus died for our sins, but he lives for our sanctification. He lives to restore our souls.

You may think no one has ever prayed for you before. But that's not true. Long before you were even conceived, Jesus began interceding with the Father on your behalf. Romans 8:34 says he is actually at the right hand of God this very moment, proactively sending prayers before you, behind you and around you. Not to protect you from an angry God, but to restore you to a loving Father.

What I'm trying to say is that Jesus is the essence of a proactive life. We are only able to be proactive towards him because he was first proactive towards us. What about you? Do you want to be a proactive disciple? Are you willing to cooperate with God's sanctification plan for your life? If so, then pray this simple little prayer. In fact, let's pray it together.

Step Five Prayer

"Heavenly Father, just like David, I want to have a clean heart and a right spirit. We both know I've made a lot of mistakes. But I truly want to cooperate with you in the sanctification of my soul. So I surrender my life my soul and my spirit to your loving arms. Redeem me according to your grace and mercy poured out for me on the Cross.

Lord, I give you permission to reveal to my heart and mind the static that's standing in the way of my relationship with you. Give me insight and revelation about the distorted unredeemed ideas that I've adopted as truth. Show me the blind spots I'm carrying around and the potential hazards they can create. And let me experience your love and tender mercies in the process.

I choose to forgive those who passed their blind spots to me and ask you forgive them as well. But I also ask your forgiveness for adopting them as my own. Deliver me from any anger and condemnation that it might provoke, knowing that it's your love that brings us all to our senses. And it's your love that will restore us all to the life you originally intended us to live.

Help me to know you as a loving Father, mentoring me on the things I don't know I need to know. Give me grace from your throne to be what I don't know I can be; the person you've predestined me to become. I asked for all of this as a free gift so that the accolades for my new life might be given to you. Amen."

Personal Reflection

Spiritual blind spots can hide in a variety of heart issues. Some heart issues include:

1. Judgments we make about life, God, ourself and other people, based on experiences.

2. Entitlements we have developed from familiar circumstances or the things we have been taught to believe.

3. Un-forgiveness concerning hurts we have been subjected to or mistakes and choices we have made.

4. Unbelief – putting more faith in the power of something or someone to be more powerful than God himself.

Ask God to shed new light on these areas as it relates to how they may have formed spiritual blind spots in your life.

_____

_____

_____

_____

_____

_____

_____

_____

_____

_____

_____

_____

Now what I am commanding you today is not too difficult for you or beyond your reach. It is not up in heaven, so that you have to ask, "Who will ascend into heaven to get it and proclaim it to us so we may obey it?" Nor is it beyond the sea, so that you have to ask, "Who will cross the sea to get it and proclaim it to us so we may obey it?" No, the word is very near you; it is in your mouth and in your heart so you may obey it.

Deuteronomy 30:11-14

SECTION TWO

THE 5 STEPS IN ACTION

UN-CER-TAIN-TY

Adjective – not ascertainable or fixed, not clearly or precisely determined

"In the year that King Uzziah died, I saw also the Lord sitting upon a throne, high and lifted up, and his train filled the temple." (Isaiah 6:1 – New King James Version)

Uncertainty is not a new phenomenon or exclusive to a particular generation or culture. It didn't start with the housing bubble, the horror of September 11, or the global financial meltdown. Uncertainty has always been an ever-present visitor to mankind. In fact, the often lauded and revered Old Testament prophet, Isaiah, experienced his share as well.

In case you are not familiar with him, Isaiah has long been considered one of the foremost figures in the Old Testament. A "Who's Who" on the short list of Major Prophets, he wrote one of the most quoted books of the Bible. He prophesied the crucifixion, death and resurrection of Jesus Christ with amazing accuracy, and was mightily used by God to influence and chastise the movers and shakers of his time. Nevertheless, he was still just flesh and blood as we are.

And he battled with his moments of panic and uncertainty just as we do.

One such moment came when his beloved King Uzziah died around 739 B.C. Now, you might be thinking, "So what? Why should the death of one king shake someone of Isaiah's stature?" To gain some perspective, it might be a good idea to review the circumstances he was dealing with.

Uzziah became the King of Judah in 791 B.C. at the tender age of sixteen. His reign endured for 52 years. Jewish tradition claims that Isaiah was a cousin to the king. For many in that region, King Uzziah was the only king they had ever known. So losing a family member and a mighty ruler must have hit Isaiah especially hard.

Uzziah was a powerful and capable king. Under most of his rule the nation enjoyed prominence and prosperity, which naturally gave the citizens a strong sense of stability, certainty and hope for the future. While other nations in the region had a much different experience, Judah flourished during King Uzziah's reign.

But with his death, all bets were off. Those who had previously threatened Judah's demise and had conquered neighboring kingdoms were circling like vultures, triangulating and strategizing a take-over they believed was well overdue. The geopolitical landscape had dramatically changed. Judah sat perfectly positioned in the collective cross hairs.

In the midst of so much chaos and uncertainty, with everything familiar and predictable out the window, with eminent destruction on the doorstep, it's no wonder we would find even the strong and faithful on their face in the Temple, crying out to God in fear and panic, as they gazed weak-kneed in to the clouded abyss of nothing and everything!

Fast forward to 2010 A.D., Atlanta, Georgia, USA. If you've never spent an evening driving aimlessly through the darkness, crying with such intensity you could barely see the road, only to end up in some random parking lot slumped over the steering wheel in gut wrenching despair, then I wonder if you have ever really lived.

Now I know this doesn't conjure up a Biblical scene of epic importance like Isaiah's encounter in the holy Temple. But I take solace in the knowledge that the Creator of the universe is no respecter of persons, and offers His loving kindness to all generations. The God who revealed himself to Isaiah wants to reveal Himself to all of us, and will use whatever venue is available, even a random parking lot.

My despairing moment of unbearable uncertainty came when I could no longer envision a future that made an ounce of sense or gave me a grain of security. Whatever I thought I could put my hope in either no longer existed or seemed no longer possible. And compared to what I thought I needed to weather the storm, my personal deficit made me feel like an ant facing a tsunami.

In my pain and terror I cried out to God, "Lord, all I have is this tiny rubber raft. But I'm facing a fierce storm that will surely capsize me under the wind and waves. I'm terrified. I know I need a larger vessel, but I have no ability to take hold of one. I can't bear this. The waves are so huge and I feel so helpless against it all."

At that very moment, in my darkest despair, I heard the Lord speak to me. "All you can see is the wind and waves. But can you also see that I am The Commander of the Wind and the Waves on YOUR behalf? You don't need a larger vessel. You need to see me bigger than the storm, holding back the waves and holding your tiny rubber raft in my hands."

Almost immediately God brought the passage from Isaiah 6:1 to my mind. He wanted me to "see also the Lord." And just like Isaiah, God wanted me to see Him, high and lifted up, seated on His throne, still in command, still in control over my life, nothing being greater than His power, nothing taking Him by surprise, nothing being able to separate me from His love. In fact, I believe He wants all of us to see Him greater than the uncertainty, greater than our weakness and difficulty, greater than the death of all we put our trust in.

There's a reason why God describes himself as someone who "changes not," someone who is the same yesterday, today and forever. As our creator, God understands our need for stability and certainty, and He wants to provide that to us as a free gift. But since He is the only true and lasting certainty, we can only have rest and confidence to the degree we have placed our lives in His hands.

Our problem is that we keep trying to find certainty from something or someone on this earth. Basically, we look for solid ground in shifting sand. Not a good idea. When God gave Isaiah such an amazing vision of Himself, it was a reminder. Although the kingdoms of this earth may be on shaky ground, God's kingdom is never shaken nor His power to save and rescue those who love Him. And when Isaiah saw God "seated on His throne" it was a message that He was still in control.

So what about you? Do you need to see God greater than what you are facing? Are you trying to navigate the impossible in a tiny rubber raft? Do you need to know The Commander of the Wind and Waves for your life?

What if we could rewrite this passage in Isaiah and customize it for your exact situation? I don't think God would mind if we applied some "here and now" issues to this timeless passage. He loves you just as He did Isaiah. He wants you to experience Him being "high and lifted up" in the dilemma you are facing. If we believe that God is the same yesterday, today and forever, then Isaiah 6:1 is relevant for us, regardless of the particulars. So let's give it a try.

- In the year I lost my job, I saw also the Lord, sitting on His throne, high and lifted up, being my all-sufficient source of provision, meeting my need in ways I had never imagined, giving me peace that passes understanding, opening doors no man can open and conquering all my fear.

- In the year my marriage ended, I saw also the Lord, high and lifted up, seated on His throne, giving me a calm assurance that in all things He was at work for my good, giving His tender mercies to carry me through each lonely hour and letting me know that He would never forsake me.

- In the year I went bankrupt, I saw also the Lord, sitting on His throne, high and lifted up, being greater than all my failure, greater than my credit score and more powerful to restore me than all my striving and fear, guiding me through the darkness and being the only future I truly need.

- In the year my life turned upside down, I saw also the Lord, sitting on His throne, high and lifted up, being my light at the end of the tunnel, giving me the faith I need just to make it through the day, carrying my burdens in my time of weakness and being my source of encouragement and hope.

- In the year I lost my home, I saw also the Lord, sitting on His throne, high and lifted up, being my everlasting source of comfort, rescuing me from the crashing waves of self condemnation and teaching me that my worth comes from knowing Him and His unconditional love for me, and not the standards of this sinful world.

• In the year betrayal made me question everything I believed in, I saw also the Lord, sitting on His throne, high and lifted up, giving me faith to believe that no weapon formed against me will prosper, teaching me that restoration is more to be desired than justice, and that favor from Him surpasses any desire of fairness from man.

Starting to get the picture? Now, let's customize the next one for your particular issue. Just fill in the blanks below. Even if you were unable to "see also the Lord" when the situation occurred, God can still redeem it and give you the ability to see Him now and each day after.

In the year that _____, I saw also the Lord, sitting on His throne, high and lifted up. Now, think about what you need from God more than anything with regard to your particular situation. Do you need faith, peace, assurance, hope, comfort, rest, a sense of belonging, or a new start? Do you need to hear his voice, see his hand, or know his presence? Just fill in the blank and then we will commit it to God in prayer.

The main thing is to fix your eyes on how big God is rather than the bigness of the issue. Use the examples I gave you to help with your answer. Fill in the spaces below with what you want or need from God. If you don't know, don't sweat it. You may need to "Think Loaves and Fishes" first. The main thing is to give it to God so he can give you something better in return, even if all you have is a clueless mind and an empty hand.

Now, let us pray together for God's help and intervention. Let us ask to be resurrected with the ability to see

Him "on the throne, high and lifted up" in our time of uncertainty.

> *Heavenly Father, All I can see is the wind and waves of my circumstance. Everyday is just another day of staring in to the abyss of uncertainty and fear. I've been trying to function and just suck it up so as not to appear unstable. But in my alone time, in the quietness of my thoughts, I am a very terrified person, gripped with the knowledge that I have no ability to save myself in this present hour or in the days to come.*
>
> *I look at what is around me, then I look at my capacity to deal with it, and I feel like an ant facing a tsunami. The truth is Lord, apart from You, we are all just ants facing a tsunami of life greater than our ability to bear it. It is for this very reason that you sent me a Savior, Jesus the Christ.*
>
> *Lord, I bring you my terrified heart, fainting from an overdose of uncertainty. I ask that it be crucified on the cross and reckoned dead. Forgive me for placing all my trust is the wind and waves instead of your greatness and love. Resurrect me to see King Jesus as The Commander of the Wind and Waves on my behalf.*
>
> *Help me to see You, high and lifted up, reigning over my circumstances, seated on the throne of my heart, ruling over the issues that concern me with grace and compassion. Lord, give me the ability to receive your love without condemnation or fear, and give me a new vision of your all-surpassing greatness at work in my life.*
>
> *In Jesus Name. Amen.*

***

"Though the mountains be shaken and the hills be removed, yet my unfailing love for you will not be shaken, nor my covenant of peace be removed, says the Lord, who has compassion on you." Isaiah 54:10

Personal Reflection

_____

_____

_____

_____

_____

_____

_____

_____

_____

_____

_____

_____

_____

_____

_____

_____

_____

_____

_____

GRACE

Noun – The influence or spirit of God operating in humans to regenerate or strengthen them.

The subject of Grace is basically the subject of God's un-searchable, all encompassing love towards mankind. As such it is impossible to fully explain or expound on its vast multiplicities in this or any writing. I have been a Christian for many years and yet the ability to fully understand the Grace of God, and rest in it, continues to be something I struggle with. That being said, my purpose in this segment is to simply share a few experiences and ideas about God's grace that have blessed me through the years. I hope it will help you and perhaps enrich your relationship with God and others.

Not too long ago, when I was drowning in an ocean of regret over a mountain of mistakes, the Lord gave me a dream. I suppose He speaks to me in dreams because I am so distracted during the day by life and living that He can't get my attention any other way. Thank God for His persistent love.

In my dream I was on an interview for a great job with a great company. Like some of you, I am an avid "T crosser" and "I dotter," (I believe some people call that anal). So interview preparation is something I take very seriously. However, in my dream, I did everything wrong you could possibly do wrong. It was truly the interview from hell!

Not only was I late for the appointment, I showed up on the wrong day. I wore the wrong clothes with mismatched shoes. I forgot to take copies of my resume and stumbled over every single question. The interviewer was combative and intrusive. He demanded that I back up all my accomplishments with overwhelming proof, which I was unable to do to his satisfaction. The entire ordeal was more like an interrogation than an interview. I think his previous job must have been "Lead Water Boarder at Gitmo."

As the conversation finally came to a merciful close, my interrogator, I mean interviewer, stood to shake my hand and surprisingly offered me the job. Talk about shocked! The unexpected outcome woke me from my slumber. It was at that moment I heard the still soft voice of the Lord speak to my heart and say, "This is what my Grace is like; when you do everything wrong, and I bless you anyway."

Does that surprise you as much as it did me? Would you expect to be hired after a performance like that? Would you hire someone after a performance like that? Maybe you're even fighting back tears at the thought of such indescribable love. The reason I was surprised by God's message is because it was totally opposite from anything I would expect from the world, or myself for that matter. In the world, everything is contingent on our performance. But God's Grace is not contingent on our performance. If it were, then it would not be Grace.

God used a simple dream to point out how I automatically assume He will be like all my earthly encounters. It made me realize that all my striving to "get it right" had created a vicious cycle of anxiety. In other words, if all my struggles to bless myself by getting it right had failed to deliver what I needed, how could I expect anything good if I got it wrong!

That conclusion, born from countless experiences, frustrations, hurts and disappointments had compromised my ability to take hold of God's Grace for me. The belief that blessing only happens if I get it right, lead to endless striving to get it right. Yet I could never "get it right enough" to attain the level of blessing and peace I needed. And even if life threw me a bone now and again, I still labored under the worry of what tomorrow would bring. What a torment. What a burdensome way to live.

Thank God he was able to penetrate my thick skull and speak to my heart about His love. Even the ability to take hold of God's Grace is an act of God's Grace. That's why Paul said, "While we were yet sinners," (unable to get anything right, blind to the fact that we couldn't, clueless that we needed a Savior and helpless to do anything about it) "Christ died for us." What an amazing salvation. What amazing Grace.

I once heard someone say that God's Grace makes provision for our mistakes much like a parent makes provision for a child. For instance, a good parent doesn't condemn a toddler because she can't run a marathon, or punish a young boy because he can't fly a fighter jet. Jesus said, "If you being evil know how to give good gifts to your children, how much more will your Heavenly Father give good things to those that ask." (Matthew 7:11) And what better gift could we possibly receive than the gift of Grace? In other words, God has already factored in a learning curve for our life.

I'm not suggesting that because of Grace we can just throw all care and caution to the wind or live any way we please and then presume on the goodness of God. I am of the opinion that once a person has truly experienced God's grace it compels them to seek him more. Even if in our ignorance we resist or reject Grace, we can never nullify it or reverse God's eternal quest to show us His love and compassion.

An insightful young pastor in Washington D.C. wrote a book entitled, "In a Pit with a Lion on a Snowy Day." He gave a truly fantastic illustration of God's grace concerning our mistakes. He recalled how in 1977, a team of IBM engineers designed a computer called Deep Blue specifically developed to outmaneuver grand chess master Garry Kasparov. Deep Blue was equipped with thirty-two processing engines, capable of calculating 200 million chess moves per second.

The author suggested that our life is similar to a game of chess. Many times we have no idea what our next move should be, but God already has the next 200 million contingencies planned out for us ahead of time. God's grace has made complete provision for our learning curve and mistakes through His infinite wisdom and love.

I believe St. Paul said it this way, "In all things God works for the good for those who love Him and have been called according to His purpose," (Romans 8:28). Or consider Psalm 37:23-24. "The Lord directs the steps of the godly. He delights in every detail of their lives. Though they stumble, they will never fall, for the Lord holds them by the hand."

The degree to which we can believe in the sovereignty of God's Grace at work on our behalf determines how we live; whether in fear, striving, anger and separation or in peace, assuredness, forgiveness and communion. Maybe some of your past decisions or present situation has stolen your peace. Maybe despair and anxiety has overtaken your heart and mind. If so, then ask a divine question such as, "What am I putting my faith in? Is it the power of mistakes and circumstances or the power of God's love and grace?"

I struggled through a very painful season where I was totally convinced I had screwed up my life beyond repair; too much loss, too many mistakes, not enough time to fix it. But God kept reminding me of Proverbs 24:16, "Though a righteous man falls seven times, he will rise again..." In Biblical numerology seven represents completeness or perfection.

So maybe this scripture is trying to tell us is that although we might feel like the "perfect" failure or believe we have blown it "completely," as the beloved of God, and by His grace, we WILL rise again. What if we stop right now and pray. It feels like the Lord is speaking to our hearts, so let's just go with it.

***

Heavenly Father, I have made a complete mess of things. I honestly don't know how I got to this place. It surely was not something I intended for myself. I never purposed in my heart to be in this predicament. I don't even recognize my life anymore. I'm angry all the time, and mostly at myself. I can't sleep, don't enjoy relationships or activities the way I used to. I'm just buried in this mire of unbelief and self-condemnation. The internal strength that once seemed so effortless has dried up and it's depressing me. I've never been a person who gives up. I'm the one who always keeps going, and going, and going. But this ordeal has totally kicked my butt, and I'm exhausted.

I guess what I am trying to say, Lord, is that I've reached the place where I can't be my own savior any longer and it's terrifying. But maybe, this is exactly where you want me. Not in terror but in a place where I can experience you being my Savior. The problem is I've never had an expectation of anyone else being there for me. That's why I became so self-sufficient; or so I thought. Now that I realize how badly I need You, my heart and mind is so crippled with unbelief, I can't take hold of faith in your love and grace to be my help and deliverance.

Lord, break the power of this unbelief and despair off my heart and mind. Forgive me for spending a lifetime trying to be my own salvation and shutting you out or minimizing your grace to be nothing more than a simple consolation prize. The truth is, You ARE the Prize. Father, give me whatever grace I need to receive you in this situation for this hour. Resurrect my heart to a new experience of your love and mercy at work in my life greater than all the mistakes. Give me rest for my soul and hope in my heart.

In Jesus Name. Amen.

Extra Points:

Can you also believe God's Grace has made provision for what someone else's decisions and mistakes have cost you? Ouch! That is a tough one, I know. However, if we believe that God's Grace is limited by what someone else does or doesn't do, we also believe that the other person has more power over our life than God.

Take a moment to Be Honest. Reflect on what you might be putting your faith in. Whether it's the power of another person's decisions or the power of God's grace at work in your life. Would you like to pray about it? If not, then skip to the next section. It's your choice as always. But before you go, try this wee little warm up prayer.

> *Heavenly Father, This is so painful right now I just can't go there. The mere thought of it makes my heart sink and my blood pressure soar. Nevertheless, I ask that your Holy Spirit would give me the grace I need to go there so I can experience You being greater than this load of junk that is plaguing my emotions.*
>
> *I bring the load of junk to the Cross and give you permission to unravel the knots in a soft and gentle way. Lord, you know my frame and character. Speak to my heart and mind so that I can put my faith in you rather than the power of another person's decisions or mistakes.*
>
> *In Jesus Name. Amen.*

Not only has God made provision for our mistakes, His Grace also empowers us in our weakness. Have you ever made the statement, "I just can't do this anymore" or "I can't handle this any longer." Guess what? That is actually a true statement. We all have moments when we can't endure anymore, can't pray anymore, hope anymore, or forgive anymore. Real life is real, and sometimes the marriage, the children, the co-workers, or that never ending difficulty and hardship drains us beyond what we can overcome in our own strength.

However, most of us never think of taking our limitations to the Cross and asking God to create something supernatural in and through us. The Bible says that in our weakness, His power is made perfect. That means that our limitations don't limit God and as long as we call on His strength, we will have more than enough to handle, endure or overcome whatever life throws at us. Just like the Loaves and Fishes illustration.

True story: When I was in my 30's I decided to return to college to complete my degree. When my guidance counselor informed me that I needed a statistics class to complete the math requirements, my heart skipped a beat. I always thought of statistics as something for brainiacs or math nerds, of which I was neither. But my guidance counselor had made it crystal clear. If I wanted the diploma, I had to pass the course.

The first week of class was truly mind numbing. If the instructor had been speaking a lost language from the jungles of South America, it could not have been more difficult. I was grasping absolutely nothing and my first test score confirmed it with a glowing F. Although my nerves were rattled, I decided to study harder and take better notes. Surely it had to improve at some point.

But after two more weeks of dumb founded blank stares and another devastating test score, the Category 5 panic set in. How could this possibly be my fault? After all, I was in the National Honor Society. My GPA was near perfection. "It must be the instructor's teaching style," I concluded.

So with bold confidence I informed him of my dilemma. "You see Sir, we are now entering the third week of class. I am studying everything you have assigned. I never miss a lecture and take copious notes. Yet I have not been able to score above a D. I am National Honor Society, scheduled to graduate Magna Cum Laude and have never struggled this much with any of my courses. It is my conclusion that your teaching style is the cause of my confusion. You simply must teach in a way that I can understand the material!"

I wish there had been a camera so I could share with you the look that young man gave me just before he shook his head and politely walked away. This was not the response I had in mind. He said nothing, offered nothing, helped me with nothing! If ever somebody's goose was cooked, mine was burned to a crisp!

I know what you're thinking. My situation was not exactly a matter of life and death. I suppose I could have sucked it up and swallowed a D for the course. But I just could not take D for an answer. I knew there had to be a solution. Up until that point I was looking for it in myself or in the hope of changing another person.

But I was coming up completely empty handed. And truthfully, it shook me more than a little bit. All my hard work, all the long hours studying to keep my GPA up, graduating with honors, all of it was falling off a cliff. And I had neither the time nor resources to turn it around.

If you ever have an opportunity to read II Chronicles chapter 20, I highly recommend it, especially verses 1-30. Without going in to much detail, let's just say that King Jehoshaphat (and with a name like that, you definitely need grace) was stuck between a rock and a hard place with no way out and no solution. But the Bible says that in the midst of his dilemma, "He inquired of the Lord." And that is exactly what I did. Driving home that evening I inquired of the Lord. In other words, I took my Loaves and Fishes and put it in the hands of a Savior.

"Heavenly Father, You are the Creator of all mathematics. Math was your idea and you have all wisdom and understanding of everything for all time. Lord, I bring you my inability to understand this course. Impart to my mind the ability to understand statistics. By the power of your grace, replace my feeble limited ability with your strength and ability in this situation. In Jesus Name, Amen."

Two days later I was back in class. As usual the instructor began his lecture with equations that took up two entire chalkboards. And, as usual, I sat there clueless and lost, understanding nothing. But I remembered my prayer and I silently "inquired of the Lord" again. "Father, give me the ability, Your ability, to understand what this man is saying. I've got nothing God. But I give it to you in faith that you will give me what I need in return."

Suddenly, in an instant, I saw it. It was like a switch was turned on and a waterfall of understanding came flooding in to my mind. I kid you not. I went from understanding nothing one second to comprehending everything as if I had always known it the next second. It took all my composure not to leap from my chair and shout for joy.

From then on, I completed the homework assignments with little to no effort. My miraculous understanding of the subject was almost entertaining. I looked forward to seeing how fast I could work an equation. On the next test I scored a B, and then A's on all the rest. I went from D and F to B and A, almost overnight. I received a perfect score on the final exam and an A for the course. The instructor actually called me a geek. It was one of the nicest compliments I had ever received.

You see, God's ability to create something from nothing isn't limited to the creation of the world. It is the embodiment of His personhood. It is the essence of Grace. God takes our nothingness, our emptiness, our end of the rope-ness and creates the capacity in our hearts and minds to receive His resources for the situations of life. We give Him our inability and He gives us His abundance. What a deal!

Romans 5:20 tell us, "Where sin abounds, grace abounds more." I like to think that it also means where our weakness abounds, or where the struggles of life overwhelm us, God's grace is available in a greater measure to overcome it for us. We simply need to ask.

Imagine if you could love your spouse by grace, raise your children by grace, work your job or be unemployed by grace, forgive yourself and others, go through the bankruptcy, suffer a great loss, overcome the addiction, or meet the unrealistic demands all by grace? Rather than fretting over circumstances or striving to change someone else, you could simply ask God for grace greater than the situation or difficulty.

I know this may sound impossible. The truth is, with man it is impossible. But with God, all things are possible. And besides, enduring in your own limited strength isn't doing you any good anyway. So why not try something different? Want to know a prayer God will always answer? Are you ready? "Heavenly Father, give me more Grace."

I guess what I am trying to say is if you don't know to call on God's grace, or you don't understand it's enabling power, then your only alternative is to live a life trying to cover yourself through striving or laboring under despair when all your striving fails to deliver what you had hoped for.

So let's take a second look at Romans 5:20 with our own individual issues and think about it this way:

- Where fatigue abounds, let grace abounds more.

- Where disappointment and regret abounds, let grace abound more.

- Where hopelessness abounds, let grace abound more.

- Where panic attacks and sleepless nights abound, let grace abound more.

- Where sickness and suffering abounds, let grace abound more.

- Where betrayal and loss abound, let grace abound more.

- Where broken dreams and broken hearts abound, let grace abound more.

Remember, our limitations are just that; our limitation. But they can also serve as a reminder to call upon the Grace of Jesus in our time of need. If it will help, feel free to use the prayer I prayed about my statistics class as a template.

> *"Heavenly Father, I bring you this painful diffi-cult situation (put your challenge here: marriage, parenting, work, finances, sickness, loss, addic-tion). Lord I am so perplexed and clueless how to fix or solve this. But you have all wisdom and understanding of everything for all time.*
>
> *Lord, I ask that by your Grace you would super-naturally impart to my life the strength, wisdom, ability and hope I need regarding this matter. I bring my weakness and inability to the cross and ask that it be crucified. Resurrect me in Jesus so I*

can replace my endless striving, failure and confusion with Your strength and grace.

Forgive me for giving up. Forgive me for looking to myself or others for what only you can provide. And forgive me for putting more faith in the bigness of circumstances as I perceive them rather than faith in the bigness of your Grace. Father, I ask that you transform my inability with Your supernatural ability for this situation.

In Jesus Name, Amen."

***

As I was writing this chapter, I began to ask God why He extends so much Grace to us. There must be something He knows about the basic necessity of Grace that we don't, and why it is so critical for our daily existence. He began to show me that in the Garden of Eden, Adam and Eve lived in a sphere of completeness, spirit, mind and body, because they lived and moved and had their being completely in God. But sin changed all that for all mankind.

The cross of Jesus was God's method of restoring what Adam and Eve lost. However, we don't have the same frame of reference for Grace or God they had. Which means we are on a life-long reconciliation path, a path we have never walked before. God knows this and He understands the struggles we face. He also never expected we could do it without Him. Grace imparts to us what we need while we are walking blindfolded in the dark on a road we've never traveled to a place we've never been.

The book of Isaiah says it is "Not by might or by power, but by my Spirit, says the Lord." In other words, it's not by our efforts, but by God's Grace that goodness and mercy follows us all the days of our lives. So let the Cross of

Jesus not only speak to you of the great sacrifice for salvation. Let it also serve as a reminder that God never expected you to live this life in your own strength.

I'm sure you have heard the over quoted phrase "Today is the first day of the rest of your life." Maybe that saying inspires you to stay focused. Maybe it gives you a sense of destiny. If so, that's great. But when I hear it my first thought is, "Holy crap, that's a lot of pressure. I better get it right today, because the 'rest of my life' depends on it." For me, a more comforting phrase would be, "Today is the first today in my life, and Gods' grace has already made provision for it." Now that's something I can rest in.

***

"And God is able to make all grace abound to you, so that in all things, at all times, having all that you need, you will abound in every good work." 2 Corinthians 9:8 (NIV)

Personal Reflection

Now it's your turn. What is presently abounding in your life where God's grace needs to abound more? Make you own list and then ask God's grace to reign over it. Take your limitations to the cross and ask Him for a specific anointing (or measure of Grace) to exceed the current challenge.

_____

_____

_____

_____

_____

_____

_____

_____

_____

_____

_____

_____

_____

_____

_____

_____

_____

STAN-DARD

Noun – a rule or principle that is used as a basis for judgment

Daniel was an aspiring resilient young man who never settled for mediocrity. Hard working and ambitious, he accomplished anything he set his mind to. Life had trained him to be a high achiever. You see, during his last year of middle school, both parents were killed in an auto accident. Daniel became the de-facto head of household for his two younger sisters. Although they lived with elderly grandparents, the girls looked to him for stability and security.

So when he decided to pursue a graduate degree in his late twenties, tackling a full time job plus a full semester of classes was no big deal. Not only did he excel at work, he also maintained a 4.0 GPA. But when his boss sold the business, the new owners cut Daniel's hours significantly. Soon after, his girlfriend took off for greener pastures, leaving Daniel holding the bag for all the living expenses.

The drastic change in circumstances resulted in a few late rent payments to a landlord who was less than understanding, and communicated his resolve with some hefty late charges. On occasion he'd get a little down in the dumps and complain to his friends, "Can't this greedy S.O.B see how hard I'm working, busting my butt to put myself through grad school, trying to improve my future? Now I'm stuck in a lease with no one to help pay for it." He would often conclude by saying, "If I am ever a Landlord, I will never treat anyone the way this cold-hearted jerk has treated me."

The cold-hearted jerk he was referring to was a man by the name of Andrew Collins. But most people just called him Mr. Andy. A tough and gruff World War II Veteran, Mr. Andy was one of five boys born to a poor family just a few miles from Clemson, South Carolina. He grew up in the depression. And like so many during that era, he worked any job he could find and sold anything he could sell just to put a few coins in his pocket.

One week after his eighteenth birthday, Andrew joined the United States Navy. He saw it as an opportunity to learn a skill with the added bonus of three meals a day and a bed. When the war ended, he moved back to Clemson and used the money he had saved to start a neighborhood plumbing business. The first couple of years were difficult. But Andrew was determined to make it.

As the business became more profitable, he started buying rental property, mostly renting to people down on their luck. Andrew knew a thing or two about that. As a child he and his family were constantly moving. A depressed economy and a father with a drinking problem often left his mother with less than enough to pay the rent. Andrew remembered the tearful desperate look on his mother's face each time they were kicked out for failure to pay. And each time Andrew would think to himself, "Can't these greedy jerks see how my family is struggling? And there is no one to help us. If I am ever a Landlord, I will never treat people like that."

But Andrew's kindness was often exploited by tenants habitually late on rent or those who did not pay at all. He had planned to use the rentals as retirement income when he could no longer run the plumbing business. So if he had any chance of paying for his investments, he had to make some serious changes. By the time Daniel came along, Andrew had perfected his game plan and was executing his late penalties and evictions without a glitch. After six straight months of late rent, Andrew refused to renew Daniel's lease and sent him packing.

Despite the setbacks, however, Daniel finished grad school with honors. True to his nature he persevered through the fits and starts and later secured a good paying job with a signing bonus. As his career grew he decided to use some of his savings to buy rental property. With a wife and family, he wanted more income and a chance to leave a few assets to his children.

Daniel mostly bought near college towns with the thought of giving working students a nice place to live for a fair price. However, not everyone appreciated his compassion, which often made him a target for the irresponsible and unreliable. He soon realized if he didn't change his approach, his assets would become cash sucking liabilities. So he adopted some very strict and punitive payment policies. Besides, the rental market was stronger than ever. The housing bubble presented more opportunity to rent to working professionals, allowing Daniel to shed the unpredictability he had experienced catering to the student demographic.

But Megan did not fit either of those categories. As a struggling single mother she had no time to grow her career, nor the money to finish college. Her adorable little boy suffered serious asthma problems, so Megan gave all her spare to him. There were no late night parties or romantic dates. But there was also no child support from her ex, which often put Megan in a very difficult position when rent was due. She always paid something, as much as she could. But the late payments were piling up and Daniel decided not to renew her lease.

She begged him to give her more time. "I'll call my ex-husband for money," she told him. "If we move, my son will have to change schools," she pleaded. "There is nothing else in the area I can afford." But Daniel had already leased the townhouse to someone else. "You need to be out by the first," he explained.

Megan was devastated. She sat on her front steps sobbing with hopeless despair. "Can't anyone see how hard I am working?" she thought. "We never cause trouble. I never ask for help and my ex never sends a dime. What kind of cold hearted person does this?"

When move day arrived, she pushed through the tears, doing her best to make it seem like a game for her little boy's sake. As they drove away, her beat up car loaded to the gills and her happy home in the rear view mirror, with a lump in her throat Megan whispered to herself, "If I am ever a Landlord…"

Daniels' story is a familiar one. Another person's actions or decisions cause hurt and frustration for someone else. The injured party judges the offender and vows in their heart to do it better. We could easily substitute the word landlord for manager, spouse, parent, coach, friend or teacher. My favorite is politician.

How often have you heard a political challenger critique the incumbent and then vow to the constituents that he or she will do it better? But soon after taking office they quickly realize their number one job is to get re-elected, which throws them in to the same circumstances and decision making as their predecessor.

As we discussed in Step 4, we all judge other people. And we all carry the demand for life and others to fit within the framework of standards we have either learned or contrived. In fact, we do it like breathing. And, similar to breathing, much of our judging and condemning is so involuntary our minds don't even realize it is happening.

Making judgments in accordance with our own standards seems reasonable, and even logical. But have you ever considered where those standards came from? Before we go any further, let me clarify that I am not talking about acts of violence or destructive behavior. What I am referring to are the everyday relational and circumstantial events that tempt our hearts towards judging based on our own set of standards.

To correctly answer the question on the origins of standards, we must first go back to the beginning, to mankind's original acknowledgement of right and wrong. The story of Adam and Eve partaking "The Forbidden Fruit" has been used in so many euphemistic ways it has almost become a fable.

But in the Biblical context, when we look at the original story, the emphasis is not on the fruit, but rather on the name of the tree that bears the fruit. To this day, no one truly knows the exact "fruit" Adam and Eve partook. But we do have a record of the tree that produced it.

It was called the Tree of the Knowledge of Good and Evil. You could also call it the Tree of the Understanding of Right and Wrong. The tempter promised if they ate from it they would, "become like God, knowing good and evil." As he so often does, Satan used a lie to propose a solution to a problem that did not exist. His goal was for Adam and Eve to exchange their relationship with their loving Father for a system of do's and don'ts.

And that is exactly what happened. Adam and Eve gained a keen knowledge of right and wrong, of do's and don'ts, along with an innate understanding of the way things should. They chose competition with God's love instead of being covered by God's love. It was the genesis of faith in false standards, of disharmony and disconnection. Genesis chapters 2 and 3, gives all the juicy details. But there was one small problem with their new insight. They possessed neither perfect love nor perfect wisdom to know how to handle it "like God."

As their descendant, we have inherited the same keen understanding of right and wrong, with the same innate understanding of the way things should be. And just like Adam and Eve, we also do not possess perfect love and wisdom to handle it like God. In so many words Satan told them the same three lies he tells us today.

The first is, "You deserve to be treated differently." (The genesis of judging people based on a standard other than God's love.)

The case of the shrewd landlord is a perfect example of how we use a standard other than God's love to judge people. Daniel, Andrew and Megan each had a standard that called for others to be understanding, compassionate, long suffering, and benevolent. All of which are noble qualities. But even the noble things of life still fall short of the Giver of Life and all He has to give.

When their experience became incongruent with their standards, it produced judgment. The judgment produced bitterness and the bitterness produced a vow that, given a similar situation, they would be able to show perfect love and wisdom just like God apart from God. Paul the Apostle wrote in Hebrews 12:15, "See to it that no one misses the grace of God and that no bitter root grows up to and cause trouble and defile many."

Andrew and Daniel eventually behaved in the same way they had judged someone else and experienced what Jesus said would happen in Matthew 7:2. In other words, the manner in which we are tempted to judge a person is most likely the same way they judged someone as well. When we do the same thing they did, we put ourselves on the same path. In other words, we begin the journey of following their footsteps instead of the footsteps of Christ.

At what point in the story could the cycle of judging and bitterness have ended? The answer is, anywhere. Because Daniel, Andrew and Megan made the attainment of a standard their salvation, they missed an opportunity to experience God. As a result they defiled each other with their unbelief. Their faith was misplaced. Their hope was in what the attainment of standards would deliver, rather than faith in God and his standard of love towards them regardless of what others might do.

The second lie is, "You need to posses something more than you presently have." (The genesis of judging our circumstances based on a standard other than God's love.)

Ingrid moved to Austin, Texas in her late thirties with her husband Marko and their two children. After building a successful career in Frankfurt Germany, they left an established pediatrics practice to be closer to family in the States. They used the move as an opportunity to tweak their career track.

Because Marko was more fluent in English, they agreed he would go back to college first. Their sacrifices were many. The time constraints and conflicting schedules took a toll on their relationship. But after months of hard work Marko completed school and was invited to join a successful sports medicine group. Ingrid was happy for her husband, but also for herself. Now that Marko's journey was complete, she could focus on re-launching her career.

But Ingrid's plans hit an unexpected speed bump when Marko later informed her he had turned down the offer in Austin, and was moving to Houston to be with a fellow student he had fallen in love with. In addition to the immense hurt and betrayal she felt, Ingrid also made several judgments about her situation.

- I screwed myself by moving to America.

- I don't have the resources to relaunch my career.

- Everyone in my family is successful. Failure is unacceptable.

- Who wants a broke middle aged woman with two children.

- I'm going to struggle for the rest of my life.

- My children will grow up without a father.

- My dreams are dead.

- My life is over.

After a few counseling sessions, she was finally willing to pray about each judgment. We discovered that many of her judgments were based on the standards she and her family had adopted. Agreeing with those standards placed her heart and mind in lock-down and blocked her from the ability to receive God's standard of love for her situation.

The standards she had been raised with made no provision for faith in a loving God, only faith in what attaining the standards would produce. Letting go of the false standards opened the door to experience faith in God's standard of love. It gave her faith to trust in his ability to restore her life and bring something better than all she had put her hopes in.

As she released her limited ideas regarding life the way she thought it would be, it freed her heart and mind to rest in God's unlimited possibility of blessing. Up to that point, all Ingrid could see was how badly she and others had missed the mark. But the only mark she had truly missed was faith to believe that nothing could separate her from the deliberate love of God at work on her behalf. Once that issue was settled, she was able to rest in the knowledge that God would open doors she had never even thought about.

She began to recall the subjects she enjoyed most while in med school, and realized it was medical research that made her the happiest. A few weeks later she landed a fantastic good paying job in pediatric disease research. Her office was close to home and the hours made it easier to juggle single motherhood and career.

After a while, she was able to forgive Marko. In the process she discovered that he had been raised with the same false standards, but to an even greater extent. Most of his life he had struggled with feelings of failure and the fear of not measuring up. The affair and the move to Houston was an unsanctified way of coping with the pressure. It did not excuse his behavior, but it did help explain it. Marko had missed out on God's standard of love for his life as well.

That realization changed Ingrid's heart from anger and revenge to love that covers a multitude of sin. Experiencing God's standard of love for herself compelled her to want the same for Marko. The more she forgave him, the easier it was to talk. Eventually, he moved back to the area and began the process of repairing the relationships and restoring the family.

A good friend once told me, "It is not so much the events that happen to us, but rather the judgments we make in response to those events that cause our lives the greatest difficulty." When we measure our circumstances against a standard void of God's love, we naturally make judgments about those circumstances, and ourselves, in a manner that is void of God's love.

His love for us is seldom a variable in the equation of our inductive or deductive reasoning. But if we don't believe God loves us, if we agree with the judgments instead of agreeing with God, what else can we do? Oswald Chambers said, "No one is ever united with Jesus Christ until he is willing to relinquish not sin only, but his whole way of looking at things."

The third lie is: "You are not good enough as you are." (The genesis of judging ourselves based on a standard other than God's love.)

When Alaskan Governor Sara Palin was selected as John McCain's Vice Presidential running mate, she hit the political landscape like a rock star. Conservatives could not get enough of her and liberals worked overtime to minimize her effectiveness. Governor Palin's influence and popularity was so electrifying, many wondered if the wrong name had been placed at the top of the Republican ticket.

As a woman, I was happy to see an accomplished female mixing it up a bit. However, my reaction to Governor Palin was slightly different than my conservative brethren. Each time I saw her on television or heard her speak, I was completely overwhelmed with feelings of condemnation and failure; so much so that I would have to change the channel or leave the room.

Mind you, it had nothing to do with what she was saying or how she was saying it. In fact I truly liked Governor Palin, and admired her success. But I could not get past the intense feeling of condemnation and failure she provoked in me. After several weeks of that experience, I decided to pray about it and called on God for help. The conversations went something like this:

Me: Lord, I don't know why this is making me feel so condemned, but you do. Show me what is causing it and why it is stealing my peace. Speak to my heart in a way that I can understand so I can experience your love instead of the condemnation.

God: What does Sarah Palin represent to you?

Me: Truthfully?

God: If you want to get rid of the pain, the truth is a good place to start.

Me: She represents everything I always wanted. It's like watching someone else live my dreams instead of me.

God: What do you mean?

Me: Well, she's successful, she's beautiful, has a big family, encouraging parents, and great friendships. And if that weren't enough, she lives in one heck of a beautiful place.

God: What have you judged it would give you if you could have everything she has?

Me: I guess… I would feel like I did something right, like I finally made it… It would make me feel like a winner and not a loser.

God: And what would that give you?

Me: It would make me feel accepted.

God: Accepted?

Me: Actually, it would make me feel acceptable.

God: Acceptable to whom?

Me: To myself… and to the world I guess.

God: And what would that give you?

Me: Peace of mind, rest for my soul…

God: But, I am the only One who can give you that. And all you have to do is ask me.

Me: …..

God: ….

Me: You're right, Lord. I'm sorry. Please forgive me.

God: I forgive you. And, when you have time, try to think about why my acceptance of you isn't enough? I'll be here if you want to talk more.

Without even realizing it, I had made Sara Palin the standard to measure my life by? While I was praying and asking forgiveness, God reminded me that I was not created in the image of someone else. I was created in His image. Comparing my life to someone else was not only foolish, but a subtle form of rebellion. Subconsciously, I was accusing God of making a mistake.

When we make someone else the benchmark for our own life, we substitute that person for God. Can you say "Idolatry?" The first century church in Corinth was apparently struggling with a similar temptation, which prompted the Apostle Paul to correct them by stating, "When they measure themselves by themselves and compare themselves with themselves, they are not wise." The New Living Translation says it this way, "But they are only comparing themselves with each other, using themselves as the standard of measurement. How ignorant!" (2 Corinthians 10:12)

Suppose Daniel, Megan and Andrew had chosen to Take an Eye Exam instead of judging and condemning. Suppose they were secure in God's love for them and truly believed their steps were ordered of the Lord, even when it did not make sense to human logic. Suppose they started asking Divine Questions that allowed them to see their experiences as an invitation from the throne of God to reconcile generations of pain; past, present and future.

I am not suggesting that you take an oath to never judge and condemn. That is an impossible endeavor this side of heaven. What I am suggesting is that you try as best you can to go to God in prayer when it happens. Recognizing false standards at work in our hearts presents opportunities for redemption, not only for ourselves but also for those who provoke us.

Some people spend their entire lives trying to nuance the universe to fit a set of standards they believe will bring them peace and security. There is a standard worth attaining, however. That standard is Love. And that Love is the person of Christ.

Heavenly Father, Just like Adam and Eve, I have exchanged a system of do's and don'ts for relationship with you. I too have put my faith in what the attainment of standards would deliver rather than faith in your love and grace for me. Jesus, forgive me. I had no idea what I was doing. I guess that why you said "Father forgive them. They know not what they do." I am so thankful that you were saying those words for me as well.

Lord, I bring to your cross all my standards born from the lies of the enemy, and ask that they be crucified. Resurrect me in Christ with a brand new ability to see myself, my situation and the people I encounter from your perspective, rather than through the prism of worldly standards.

Thank you for providing a way of escape from the curse of the Garden through your death and resurrection. I give you permission to speak to my heart concerning things you want me to rethink or reconsider. And give me whatever measure of grace I need to live a brand new life. Amen.

***

"And my God shall supply all of your needs according to his riches in glory in Christ Jesus" (Phillipians 4:19 – New American Standard)

Personal Reflection

_____

_____

_____

_____

_____

_____

_____

_____

_____

_____

_____

_____

_____

_____

_____

_____

_____

_____

_____

DI-REC-TION

**Noun – A purpose or orientation toward a goal
that serves to guide or motivate**

Me: I don't know what to do about this Lord.

God: What do you mean?

Me: Well, I don't know what I should do about
      my situation.

God: Who told you that you should do something?

Me: …

God: …

Me: That sounds familiar.

God: …

Me: It sounds a lot like the question you asked
      Adam and Eve.

God: That's because you have the same problem
      they had.

Me: Which is?

God: You're stuck on turning to this world or
      yourself for peace and security.

Me: Well, there is a pragmatic side to life.

God: So, pragmatism according to the world is your salvation?

Me: Well I can't just sit here and do nothing!

God: Why not?

Me: …

God: …

Me: Because something needs to be done.

God: For what purpose?

Me: For what purpose? … I guess to hedge against a painful outcome.

God: So hedging on the future is your salvation?

Me: Look, there's a freakin big avalanche headed in my direction. If I don't do something I'm going to get buried by this thing!

God: How do you know that?

Me: Is that a trick question?

God: …

Me: … Okay, I guess I am basing it on a really big mountain of experience!

God: So… you're putting all your faith in a mountain of experience?

Me: Sigh…

God: …

Me: That's all I know to do. Seriously, it's all I know to do.

God: How can you see Me if all you see are your experiences?

Me: Darn it!

God: What's the matter?

Me: … I'm just so freaking afraid.

God: What are you afraid of?

Me: How much time do you have?

God: Is that a trick question?

Me: I'm afraid of being abandoned in my time of need; I'm afraid of being wiped out by things I can't control; Of having no one to turn to; Of being so confused I can't think straight; I'm afraid of making another stupid mistake.

God: I love you. I truly love you.

Me: God, I don't mean to sound ungrateful, but exactly HOW is that supposed to help me right now?

God: You don't believe it do you?

Me: Sigh…

God: Why can't you trust that I'll take care of what concerns you?

Me: Honestly?

God: Yeah, honestly.

Me: I guess because I've spent my whole life turning to myself for answers.

God: Why?

Me: Because there was no one else to turn to???

God: Really?

Me: … Looks like I've never gave You a chance, did I?

God: Now we're getting somewhere.

Me: But it's always been up to me to find a solution!

God: Says who?

Me: Says the whole freaking world, says rugged individualism, says a lifetime of being taught that.

God: Well, maybe it's time for something else.

Me: There's just so much uncertainty, so much at stake and so much pressure to make a right decision. It's more than I can bear. I just can't do this anymore!!!

God: I never expected that you could. That's why I sent you a Savior.

Heavenly Father, Forgive me for putting all my faith in what a mountain of experience has taught me rather than faith in You. I don't know how to stop it. I've spent my entire life turning to self or the voices of the world in search of direction, comfort and help.

My pride has factored you completely out of my decision-making and reinforced a lie that You can't be trusted. I've made myself a stranger to Your love, which is the one thing I need the most. Forgive me for my unbelief and the subtle accusations my heart continually makes against you.

I ask that this mountain of experience, void of your grace, would be crucified on the cross. Resurrect me in Jesus to have a completely new experience and help me to know you for who you truly are, and not who I have judged you to be.

I give you permission to lead me and guide me so that I can experience you in the midst of my difficulty. Give me a new revelation of the love in your heart for me.

In Jesus Name, Amen.

***

I tell you the truth, if you have faith even as small as a mustard seed, you could say to this mountain (of experience), 'Move from here to there,' and it would move. (Matthew 17:20)

Personal Reflection

FAITH

Noun – confidence or trust in a person or thing.

It's perplexing how something as fundamental as faith can be so confusing and illusive. It's not as if we can buy faith on the internet. There's no Faith App, no Groupon for faith. Ask 100 people what faith is and you'll get 300 answers. Could it be we're making it harder than it needs to be? Could it be we're putting the cart before the horse? Could it be that much of the confusion and ambiguity stems from what we are told to focus on?

The predominant theme of most faith discussions focuses on the expression of faith and the promised benefits. We are told that doing certain things will help us achieve certain outcomes; that great faith depends on how successfully we demonstrate it, claim it, speak it, stand in it, walk in it, rest in it, read about it, talk about it, and invest in it.

But how do you know what to do when? What expression is best for a given circumstance? How do you know when to walk in faith or stand in faith? How can we determine when to rest or wrestle in faith? How can we know when our expressions make us seekers of results or seekers of

God? Are we creating a faith that is easily shaken or faith that is built on the Rock?

The challenge with an expression focused faith is similar to the conundrum that problem solving prayers create. Although it promises to produce faith, in reality it keeps us distracted from the activity that actually does produce faith. Think about it this way. Jesus said if we have faith the size of a mustard seed we can move a mountain. I don't know about you, but sometimes the pressure to come up with an expression of faith to prove my faith can feel like the opposite; like I need an entire mountain just to move a mustard seed.

What seems to be missing is a balanced focus on the actual origin of faith; where faith comes from and how it's formed in us? Romans 10:17 explains that, "Faith comes by hearing, and hearing by the word of God." The Greek translation for "word" as it is used in Romans 10:17 is Rhema, which literally means to utter or speak. So we could interpret the passage to say, "When we experience God's voice speaking to us in our situation, according to our frame and character, hearing his Word(s) produces the ability to trust him, to have faith in him and to act on it as he leads and guides."

In John 10:27, Jesus provides the perfect example of this. He said, "My sheep hear my voice, and I know them, and they follow me." The sheep hear the shepherd's voice because they are close to him. When they hear his voice they know they can trust what the voice is instructing. Their expression, if you will, is born from relationship, which puts them in the position to hear the trusting voice of a trustworthy shepherd. The faith to follow him, the faith needed to take action comes from the ability to hear the Voice of faith.

There are two primary avenues for hearing God. The first comes from reading the Holy Scriptures. As we discussed in Step 5, a proactive disciple makes scripture reading a part of their daily routine. Reading God's Word helps us get to know him. It lets us become familiar with his personality, his goals and plans for us and the world. Soaking in the Scriptures builds our faith in the love of God, the grace of God, the mercy of God, the greatness of God, the power of God, and the goodness of God at work in our life. It helps us rest from striving or the temptation to manufacture a pseudo faith in order to feel significant.

The second comes through prayer and meditation. The entire goal of this book is to provide you with tools and techniques to improve your prayer life. Spending time with God in prayer strengthens our relationship with him. The more time we spend in prayer the more connected we are with his heart. Not only does it help us more easily recognize his voice, it also helps us recognize a voice that is not his.

Many prominent biblical figures are routinely heralded as larger than life because of their great faith. They are sometimes presented as Super Heroes because of the things they accomplished and circumstances they overcame by faith. While their expression of faith has served to comfort and challenge generations, it's important to remember that they were no different than us in many ways. The power that propelled them forward came from their ability to hear God's voice concerning the situation or challenge.

I can't tell you exactly what God will say to you or how he will say it. Only he knows what you need to hear and how you need to hear it. Only he knows how to speak to your heart in a way that will get your attention and help you grow. But I can tell you what experiencing God's voice will NOT be like.

- When God speaks it will never be in opposition to his written Word or his character. If you need help verifying something you believe has said to you, consult with a mature believer or clergy member. Together you can test it against the scriptures.

- When God speaks, His Words are not laced with subtle manipulations or spin. In other words, He won't make you feel pressured, hoodwinked or used.

- When God speaks, His Words are not camouflaged with selfish motives or hidden agendas. God won't put you on a guilt trip to please Him. He doesn't need to be needed. He's not co-dependent.

- When God speaks, His Words don't sting with criticism, judgment or condemnation. God takes no pleasure in condemning us. It is His loving kindness that draws us. That is not to say He won't make us feel uncomfortable. Faith does challenge us. But even that presents an opportunity for conversation with God.

- When God speaks, His Words don't contain a never-ending list of demands. God doesn't require our performance. We don't have to meet certain secular or religious criteria to hear His voice. God wants our hearts to find rest in Him.

- When God speaks, His Words don't make us feel like an obligation or nothing more than a tax write off. Others may have caused you feel like that, but God doesn't demand that we make His life comfortable or convenient. The cross of Jesus was not comfortable or convenient. Yet He willing bore it to reconcile us to the Father.

- When God speaks, His doesn't' make us feel like we're walking through a land mine. God is the same yesterday, today, and forever. He's not like us, or the other people we know. He's not fickle, argumentative or combative. God doesn't require us to parse our words or trap us in some sort of conversational jujitsu. Talking with God isn't about who wins or loses. He's not "out to getcha."

Faith is not something that we consume or use as a tool to gain our desires. It's not a switch we turn on or off. Our ability to attain faith is not contingent on how well we express it. Faith is what is formed in us as we experience God's voice speaking to us; situation-by-situation, point-by-point. Faith is the work of God in us, not the work of us in us. Our participation is to ask for revelation on the obstacles that block us from hearing his voice. True faith is not outcome based. True faith is relationship based.

Dr. Crawford Loritts says it this way, "Faith is not about coming up with a bunch of ideas for God to bless. Faith is about trusting God for what he initiates in us and then walking it out." Asking for a greater ability to hear God's voice should be our first step of faith. Focusing on how to improve our relationship with the Father should be our greatest expression of faith. And it starts by following the admonition of Saint Paul in Hebrews 12:2, "Looking unto Jesus, the Author and Finisher of our faith."

Heavenly Father,

A lot of things have distorted my ideas about faith; what it means, what it looks like and most of all, where it comes from. Forgive me for making faith about the pursuit of results rather than a pursuit of you. Resurrect me to have a greater understanding of what it means to walk in faith, to pray by faith and to live by faith. Most of all I ask for a greater ability to hear and know the Voice of faith. Amen.

Personal Reflection

BUR-DENS

Noun – To weigh down, oppress or overload

Note to self: If you decide to become a follower of Jesus Christ, at some point He will take you outside your comfort zone and asked you to do something a bit unusual or something that will disarm your self confidence. He may even ask you to go somewhere you really do not want to go. Why, you ask? Because it will force you to depend on Him, it will force you to walk by faith and not by your own limited understanding. And because once God finds someone attuned to hear his voice, He will give that person some very important assignments which, on the surface may seem meaningless and superfluous, but to God, they mean a great deal.

The Father's will is that everything in the heavens and the earth be reconciled back to Him the way it was in the beginning. So if He is in the process of reconciling your life, then He will ask you to join Him in His reconciliation plan for all mankind. By the way, he gets to decide where and when and with whom that will happen. Not because He's a control freak, but because He knows every detail of each person's life. And He will match your life's journey with someone else's need. In other words, we are called to comfort others with the comfort we have received (2 Corinthians 1:4).

***

God occasionally visits me in my dreams to show me something He wants me to pray about, or tell me something He wants me to do. In one such dream the Lord asked me to go to the University of Aberdeen. I suppose a Godly person would have responded by saying, "Thy will be done Lord." But my first response was, "Why the heck would I want to do that?"

I'm middle aged, married and broke. Besides, there are plenty of Universities I could attend where I live." It made no sense to me. So I ignored it and wrote it off as a case of bad pizza.

One month passed and the same message came to me a second time. And so I committed it to prayer. Again I asked God why he wanted me to go to school in Scotland. His reply was, "I don't want you to attend the school. I want you to go to the school and the city to pray." God, in case you haven't noticed I'm broke. My husbands' business is down by 60 percent and I don't have a job. Can't I just download some pictures and pray in my living room?

Three weeks later, in early March, I was flying over the North Sea on my way to… you guessed it, Aberdeen Scotland. The trip was amazingly easy with little to no hassle. Typically I dread long flights. I am so high energy that the thought of being confined in a capsule for 9 hours makes me grouchy and board. But on this flight I felt relaxed and excited. It was the fastest nine-hour flight of my life. Though I was unsure about what I was supposed to do or pray when I got there, I truly felt God's grace for the journey and whatever was ahead.

As we entered Scottish airspace my easy-going flight took an abrupt reversal. Without warning, I was suddenly and forcefully overcome with an unbearable sense of despair and hopelessness. It was so severe it took my breath away. It literally felt like the despair was pulling in to a black hole and there was nothing I could do to stop it. I just sat there on the plane, doubled over in agony, weeping un-consolably for the remainder of the flight, while trying as best I could to hide my tears and the pain.

After we landed, I composed myself enough to make it through customs and collect my luggage. The remainder of the day was a complete struggle. I barely had an appetite and spent much of the evening sitting in the floor of my hotel room sobbing to the point of exhaustion. I was so confused by what was going on. Did I make a mistake? Did I miss God? Was I having some sort of panic attack? I had no idea what to do with that much despair. It was nothing short of horrible, and all I could think about was how to escape from it, even if it meant returning to the airport for the next flight home.

Thankfully, later in the evening, I was finally able to sleep, though it was very short lived. About 3 a.m. the Lord awakened me. With the storm of emotions subsided, He simply and quietly spoke to theses words, "The despair has no place to go, because the people have chosen to bear their own burdens."

In an instant I knew why I had been so overwhelmed with pain. God had allowed me to feel what it is like when the pain has no outlet, when it has no where to go. What He spoke to my heart combined with the experience of ravaging despair gave me the exact prayer I was sent to pray. So, in the wee hours of the morning God lead me to pray a very simple but powerful prayer. It went something like this;

Heavenly Father, On behalf of this city, I ask that you would forgive the people for believing that they have to bear their own burdens. Forgive them for the various ways they have tried to provide a solution to their own pain apart from you. The fact that I can feel it so strongly is because I have done the exact same thing.

Lord, I ask that you forgive us for not turning to you with our burdens. Forgive us for not casting our cares on to Jesus. Forgive this city and the students on this campus for all the ways they have tried to cope with burdens instead of giving them to you. The alcohol, the drugs, the hopelessness, the despair, the nasty attitudes, the multiple addictions and disorders they are suffering with are simply a result of vain attempts to be their own salvation. Lord I ask that all these coping mechanisms would be crucified on the cross of Christ and made completely dead.

Father, you never intended for these people or any people to bear their own burdens. You sent Jesus to do that job. So I ask forgiveness for our unbelief in your grace and mercy. Resurrect this city and its people to a new life in Jesus so they can take hold of Christ being their Burden Bearer for every pain and care. In Jesus name Amen.

I am always amazed by God's heart for His world and the hurting people who live in it. There is no length He will not go to in order to answer the prayers of those in need, even if it means sending one clueless bumbling struggling American across the ocean to pray one prayer for one city. And he orchestrates situations in such a way that there can be no mistake that it is His divine purpose at work.

Before my trip to Scotland, I had never really understood how much Jesus not only desires to bear our burdens, but, is the only person with the capability to do so. We were never created with a burden bearing capacity. God did not create us to bear our own burdens, although he does sometimes give us the grace to bear those of others. But it is always for the purpose of intercession.

Think about it this way; if we could bear our own burdens then we would. And if that is true then we should also have the capacity to bear them in such a way that they aren't burdensome. And if that's true then we wouldn't feel stressed and weighed down. We wouldn't be addicted to a pill, a bottle, or a pipe. We wouldn't have to struggle with despair, abusive behavior, panic attacks or any other coping mechanism just to make it through the day.

In Matthew 11:30, Jesus describes what it is like when we experience him carrying our load. He said, "My yoke is easy, my burden is light." But what does that mean? W h e n we try to carry our own burdens our minds and emotions are continuously weight down. We spend so much mental and emotional energy trying to problem-solve and strategize our own salvation. We truly believe that we are somehow a variable in the equation of our own deliverance.

But that belief system only results in frazzled nerves, fatigue, irritability, stress, anger, destructive habits or just numbing out all together. Think of it as exhaustive weight lifting on your mind. Just like a muscle, we can only bear so much weight before the muscle fatigues and gives out. When we put the weight down, our muscles feel relieved and are able to rest from the strain. That is exactly what giving our burdens to Jesus is like. When we cast the cares of our life on to Him, it takes the strain off of us and puts it on someone who was actually designed to bear it.

Now before you buy in to the notion that you are somehow a loser if you don't carry your own load, consider this. How many burdens did Adam and Eve carry before they sinned? How many did they carry after they decided to live apart from God? You see God wants us to have the same relaxed peaceful heart and mind that Adam and Eve had when they were with Him. He carried all the load for them and wants to carry all the load for us. Our job is to simply realize that it is not our job and that God does not judge us as a failure when we can't.

Each time we decide to bear our own burdens, at least three things happen. (1) We reinforce a lie from the enemy that we should or could do a God thing apart from God. That is the same old lie Satan tempted Adam and Eve with… same song, different verse with your name on it. (2) Believing the lie blocks us from experiencing the love and grace of God to carry our load. (3) We use coping mechanisms as a substitute for God's power at work on our behalf.

But you might say, "Isn't it irresponsible not to carry my own load?" Actually it is more irresponsible to judge that your ability is somehow greater than Gods'. If we could bear our own burdens, then technically they wouldn't be a burden. Don't misunderstand. I am not suggesting that we shrug off the daily activities of life that require our time and attention. I'm talking about the way we let the problems and difficulties of life, the worry and stress of life, the set backs and disappointments of life to weigh us down or tempt us to believe we have to provide for our own security, peace of mind and hope for the future.

You may also be thinking, "How could I possibly turn that much of my life over to someone I can't see? How do I know He will actually take care of the things that concern me?" Believe it or not, that is exactly where you start. God knows you don't know Him and He knows you don't trust Him. But it is His job to show His faithfulness toward you. It is your job to tell him your fears and confess your unbelief so you can receive His love in return.

What burdens have you been trying to carry? What unbearable pain are you suffering because someone or something convinced you that you are suppose to be your own burden bearer? What addiction or emotional trauma are you going through because you have tried to bear your own burdens, past, present or future, and just can't do it?

During my trip to Scotland, God allowed me to bear in my emotions a very small portion of the sorrow and despair of one city, and it was truly more than I could handle. But God sent Jesus to bear every burden, not just for Aberdeen but for every city, for every individual, for all of time. That is exactly what he did on the cross.

If you have never felt a need to praise and worship the goodness and mercy of God, then take a moment and think about his un-searchable greatness in being our burden bearer and what it cost Jesus to become the One who bears ALL our burdens, ALL the time. The lyrics to a very old hymn say, "My sin (burdens), oh the bliss of this glorious thought. My sin not in part, but the whole, was nailed to the cross and I bear it no more. Praise the Lord! Praise the Lord, oh my soul!

So, let's get the ball rolling? After all, what do you have to lose other than a load of burdens? I'm not suggesting that one prayer will fix everything. We learned that in Step One. But you have to start somewhere.

> *Heavenly Father, I bring the burdens of my life to the cross. They are truly more than I can handle. But you already knew that, which is the exact*

reason you gave me a way of escape through your Son Jesus.

In an effort to provide my own sense of security, peace and well being, I have taken on a multitude of burdens you never intended for me to bear. Father, forgive me for believing that I could be or should be my own burden barer. I really did not know what I was doing. Everyone around me does the same thing. I never knew I had a choice. Thank you for loving me and covering me in my ignorance and providing a way of escape before I even knew I needed it.

Enable me by your grace to truly cast all my care on to Christ. And even though I don't completely understand what that means, as an act of faith I commit it to you anyway. Transcend my limited understanding and open the door of my heart and mind to receive what you have for me.

Lord, as an act of my will, I chose to trust you to take care of the things that concern me, and I give you permission to show me all the reasons why I don't. Resurrect me in Jesus with the capacity to more easily believe upon you. Help me to trust that you will work out the details of my life in the ways that are best and for my good.

Continue to show me all the places I am trying to bless myself or provide for my own salvation. Father, I ask for a new heart and mind that I may take hold of what I need from you. Create in me something that does not presently exist so I can experience your kingdom, not only in this life, but also in the life to come. In Jesus Name, Amen.

***

Casting the whole of your care (all your anxieties, all your worries, all your concerns, once and for all) on Him, for He cares for you affectionately and cares about you watchfully. I Peter 5:6

Extra Points:

When my son was born and as he grew up, the best part of my life was spending time with him. Looking back, I probably enjoyed it exponentially more than he did.

Regardless of the circumstances, he NEVER felt like a burden to me. Even if grades were not as good as they could have been, even when he came home past curfew, and even when his brakes failed sending the bumper of his red 1965 Mustang through the wall of my newly painted living room three days before Christmas, he never felt like a burden.

In spite of all the ups and downs, the setbacks and daily hassles, I always felt like the luckiest person on earth to have been given such a wonderful and beautiful child. Thankfully, to this day, he tells me he always felt loved. And I thank God for his gracious blessing. Yet, not everyone was made to feel that way by their caregivers.

Maybe you were one of those people who, no matter what you did, no matter what the circumstances, no matter how small the request, somehow you always felt like a burden to others. How can a person who feels like a burden feel the freedom to ask for anything? How could you possibly have the faith to ask for guidance or help to carry the load?

For as long as I can remember both my parents expressed how proud they were that I never asked them for anything. Since all children want to please their parents, those comments put me in a trap. If I wanted to continue making my parents proud, I had to continue not asking for anything. No matter how badly I needed help, I couldn't ask because of the fear of being judged as a burden.

It took years for me to realize that God did not have those same thoughts toward me. He pronounced "good" over my life because of what Jesus did on the cross, not because of me. And he pronounces the same thing over your life if you have accepted His Son as your Savior. Maybe similar experiences have prevented you from calling on God in your time of need. If so, then the next prayer is especially for you.

Heavenly Father, For as long as I can remember, my life has felt like a burden to others. The pain of that experience tempted me to judge that I have to deal with the burdens of life alone. The thought of asking for help and then having it denied is more painful than carrying the burdens.

Those experiences ensnared my heart. They prevented me from understanding just how much you love me and desire that I cast my cares on to you.

Father, forgive me for judging that you are just like everyone else. Give me a new frame of reference for You being not only my Burden Bearer, but also the Lover of my soul. In Jesus Name, Amen.

Personal Reflection

_____

_____

_____

_____

_____

_____

_____

_____

_____

_____

_____

_____

_____

_____

_____

_____

_____

_____

_____

_____

GOLD-EN ER-A

Noun – any period of great peace, happiness and prosperity; any flourishing and outstanding period

"To everything there is a season, a time for every purpose under heaven." (Ecclesiastes 3:1)

There was a very special season in my life that lasted almost 15years. After a long and difficult period as a struggling single mother, I married a very kind man who took on the role of father to my son and treated him as if he were his own. We lived in a nice home in a wonderful neighborhood, and developed strong connections with the community, schools and church. My husband and I were blessed with good jobs and seldom stressed over money. I am not saying we were millionaires or that everything was perfect. But it was the best my life had ever been and definitely more than I could have imagined.

Never before had I felt such a strong sense of purpose, of belonging, of home and a happy future. I no longer worried about my son's well being or if I could afford the basic necessities. My husband made me feel loved and appreciated, which was also was a new experience. We shared the same values and worked towards the same goals to make our home and family a refuge of comfort.

With each passing year the happy memories grew stronger, our connections grew deeper and the stable peaceful environment I had always hoped to give my son was actually coming to pass. It was as if the desires I had as a child were being fulfilled, even to the smallest detail. I never dreamed my life could be that enjoyable. You might say it was my personal Golden Era.

But, as the old saying goes, "nothing lasts forever." Through a series of unimaginable circumstances everything began to change. Just as fall gives way to winter, my golden season transitioned to a series of setbacks and heartache. The era of life so fulfilling became like a distant foggy road in the rearview mirror. I suppose you could call it my WTH era. At least that was the phrase I seemed to use repeatedly during that time.

Ecclesiastes 3 says, "To everything there is a season, a time for every purpose under heaven." I suppose that also means a time for a Golden Era and a time for it to end. But it doesn't have to be The End, although sometimes it can certainly feel that way.

When circumstances change, especially when it is unexpected, it can feel like a kick down the road or a kick in the gut. When life makes us feel like a pinball ricocheting from tornado to hurricane to earthquake, it's hard to imagine that God is still in control. We seldom consider that he might be using the unplanned chaos to push us forward and upward.

Think of it like this, if there is a season for every purpose, then there has to be a purpose for every season. Just as snow is designed for winter, God has designed a particular purpose and grace for each season we walk through. And since it is usually for that particular season, we can't carry it in to the next any more than we can carry the snow of winter in to the heat of summer. Can you imagine wearing your favorite winter coat on summer vacation to the beach? No matter how much it blessed you during winter, the hot and humid beach weather requires something different. Summer is a new season. It has a different purpose.

When I was out for a walk one evening, I clearly heard the Lord tell me that I was never going to have the life I once had, no matter how I struggled to reinvent it. "But" he said, "That doesn't mean you can't have a great life. I'm trying to give you something new, something better. If you want it, you have to let go of the old season first."

From my perspective, my Golden Era was the best my life had ever been. But it did not mean it was the best my life would ever be. God wanted me to go forward with a new life for a new season. But the old one had to die first.

On my knees, in gut-wrenching pain (and I don't use that phrase lightly), I took the good times, the good memories and the good experiences to the cross in prayer. Not because they were bad, but because I had allowed how good it was to become an idol in my heart. Without a crucifixion, there can be no resurrection. Being resurrected to something better was the thing I desperately needed. This is what I prayed:

> *Heavenly Father, Thank you for the way you blessed me during a wonderful season of life. Thank you for the special memories, for the happiness and how much it filled my heart with joy. All of it was a gift from you to me for that particular season. But Father, in my ignorance I allowed a Golden Era to define me. I've looked to it for secu-*

rity and meaning instead of looking to you. Lord, forgive me.

As an act of my will I offer up to you my Golden Era and ask that it would be crucified on the cross. Forgive me for allowing how good it was to become an idol in my heart that competes with how great you are.

Break the power of this idolatrous affection off my heart and mind. Resurrect me in Christ to move forward to a new grace for a new day. Give me faith to trust you… to trust in your love for me as I walk in to the unfamiliar. Give me your power so I can rest in the knowledge that although the seasons of life may change your goodness towards me never changes. In Jesus name, Amen.

It seems a silly proposition to repent of enjoying something good, especially when it seems so normal and sinless. After all, doesn't God want us to be happy? Doesn't he want us to enjoy life? As long as we're not hurting anyone else, what's the big deal? Actually, God wants us to know him and to grow in our willingness to place all our hope and all our trust in Him. Not just in the physical sense but also emotionally and psychologically, from cradle to grave and every stop in between.

The divine question we need to ask is, "Are we looking for meaning and validation in a particular season of life or from The Giver of Life?" Think of it this way. If a Golden Era could truly meet the needs of our heart, why would we need a Savior?

We see this played out all around us; in marriages and families, in communities and ministries, in businesses and careers. Sometimes we allow a certain era of life to define our life or give us such a strong sense of meaning and identity that we can't imagine living apart from it. None of us do it on purpose. It is more the sin of ignorance and desperation than anything else.

If left unchecked, however, the comfort received from a particular season can become an idol that overtakes our thinking, our focus and all our hopes and dreams. Because our flesh-nature desires the familiar more than God, the imprint of a wonderful season has the potential to entomb us and impede our ability to move forward. That is exactly what happened to me, and I was completely ignorant to it.

When we make a past season of life (or a desired season of life) the pinnacle season of life, it becomes the standard we measure everything else against. It causes us to operate with a closed mind. It creates discontent and discord with people and situations. It prevents us from noticing the countless blessings surrounding our lives today.

It's easy to believe that God would desire we transcend the setbacks of life. He is and always will be our "shelter in the time of storm." Few of us, however, stop to consider that the he also wants us to transcend the Golden Eras as well. As fulfilling and comforting as they may be, the good seasons still fall short of who God is and all he wants to do in and through us. I believe God's true desire is that we live in a Divine Era in our hearts and minds, regardless of what may be happening in the natural world around us.

That is where true peace and contentment lies. It's not found in obtaining a Golden Era or trying to side step a WTH Era. It can only be found when our spirits are connected to His Spirit – when we come to a place of knowing that no matter what season we find our self in, Gods love has already gone before us, and nothing can separate us from it.

That is what St Paul was referring to in Philippians 4:11-13, "for I have learned to be content whatever the circumstances. I know what it is to be in need, and I know what it is to have plenty. I have learned the secret of being content in any and every situation, whether well fed or hungry, whether living in plenty or in want. I can do all things through him who gives me strength."

Believe me. I am not tying to downplay the trauma that accompanies rapid change or a slow spiral. It can be mind numbingly terrifying! One day your life makes sense, the next day you're fighting to just keep your sanity. I've been there on more than one occasion.

I know what it's like to lose a job. I know what it's like to lose a business or two. I am intimately familiar with having friends and family treat you with disdain because you don't meet their expectations. I know what it's like to lose a loved one. I've also experienced the sense of failure and detachment that comes with losing a home.

Did I mention bankruptcy? Got that one covered also. No matter the circumstances that cause it, filing for bankruptcy is not something anyone plans for. I have never met a single person who includes bankruptcy in their plans or contingency plans for life. I have yet to see Bankruptcy on anyone's Bucket List. Nevertheless, stuff happens.

In the days leading up to my bankruptcy, I had been praying about all the different things I had put my hope in other than the grace and love of God. The list was VERY long and it was not an easy process. Let's just say I have a new appreciation for Paul's admonition in Philippians 2:12, to "work out your salvation with fear and trembling."

My list of divine questions included things like, "Does my credit score open doors or does God open doors?

Is my worth calculated through success and advancement or in the cross of Jesus? Was this my ultimate failure in life, or an opportunity to receive a greater grace than I had ever known?"

The evening before my appointment to sign the final papers, I experienced something from the Lord I had never encountered. Although I slept like a baby, that was only part of the miracle. The best part was actually feeling the Spirit of God himself hovering over me for the entire evening.

I truly have no words to describe what it felt like. Yes, it was supernatural, but it was more than that. It was transcendent. I awoke the next morning with an indescribable unshakable sense of peace and assurance. I knew, in the deep recesses of my heart, that the God who spoke the universe in to existence had also spoken me into existence and that he had a custom designed future with my name on it. Regardless of the setbacks, no matter the season, God still had a purpose for my life.

The bridge from fear and doubt to faith and peace in God is like going from darkness to light, from confusion to order; from not knowing what your future holds or what your purpose is, to finding meaning, direction and hope. Genesis 1 says, "In the beginning God created the heavens and the earth," It describes the earth as being without form and empty, without purpose or direction; a place where darkness hung like a thick veil over everything; the past, the present and the future.

The scriptures say that the Spirit of God began to hover over the waters. As if he were comforting the shapeless, directionless, suspended nothingness and saying, "Don't worry or fret. Be not anxious about your future. Your darkness is the canvass on which I will bring forth my divine plan and purpose for you." And then God said, "Let there be light," and there was light. With a word creation was transformed by it's Creator and found its fullness in the sustaining grace and love of God.

You are his predestined creation. Regardless of how you came to be, your life is not an accident. The season you're walking through may be filled with darkness. Your future may seem shapeless and undefined. But the God who hovered over the shapeless darkness of a world yet to be wants to hover over your life as well. The majestic Creator who named every star in every galaxy has a marvelous plan for your life.

Shortly before I completed this book, my mother died from the complications of a stroke. Earlier in the year I had purchased tickets to the Broadway play "Mary Poppins," at The Fox Theatre in Atlanta. As fate would have it, my mother's funeral fell on that same day. Assuming I wouldn't be in the right frame of mind I considered giving the tickets to my friend. But I felt a strong leading from the Lord not to change my plans. It seemed God wanted me to go to the play.

And so, after her memorial I met my friend at The Fox Theatre to enjoy an evening of singing, dancing and laughter. As you can imagine, I felt a bit awkward and my emotions were quite jumbled. I knew God wanted me to be there, but the situation didn't fit in to what I would have judged as the normal way of things.

Several weeks later I was praying about why the Lord had pressed me to go to the play. He reminded me of all the times I had gone to The Fox as a child with my family and I recalled my very first visit there. It was 1964. My mother planned a special outing for the family. She and my dad took us downtown Atlanta for shopping, a special lunch and then to the majestic Fox Theatre to see Disney's latest box office hit… Mary Poppins.

Truthfully, I was stunned by that realization. Was there something symbolic about Mary Poppins' life – some meaning in the story that I had missed? Was it a matter of closure? The more I prayed about it, I realized it was none of those things. It was simply my loving Heavenly Father giving me a wink and a nod to remind me of his sovereignty and guidance through all the seasons of my life, even to the most intricate detail.

Psalm 139 is one of my absolute favorite scriptures. I like to read it when life feels lonely and confusing; when I'm buffeted with doubt and despair; when seasons change and my heart is filled with uncertainty about the future. It's comforting to know that someone else struggled along those same lines. But David broke through on the realization of God's greatness and love towards him. It reads:

> *"Where can I go from your Spirit? Where can I flee from your presence? If I go up to the heavens, you are there; if I make my bed in the depth, you are there. If I rise on the wings of the dawn, if I settle on the far side of the sea, even there your hand will guide me, your right hand will hold me fast. If I say, "Surely the darkness will hide me and the light become night around me," even the darkness will not be dark to you; the night will shine like the day, for darkness is as light to you." Psalm 139: 7-12*

I don't know what season you are presently in or what era has captured your hope and aspirations. Maybe you feel tossed about by circumstances or lost in a dense fog of uncertainty and confusion. Maybe a past Golden Era or a future longing evolved in to an idol that ensnared your heart. Whatever your situation, God desires for you to encounter his love to such a degree that it supersedes the challenge. He wants to move you forward and upward to a Divine Era that will never fade or pass away. If that sounds like something you need, then pray this simple prayer.

Heavenly Father, Forgive me for being such a knucklehead about the different season of my life. I'm so thankful you died on a cross for knuckleheads. Thank you for the blessings you have given me through the years. Thank you for special memories, for the happy moments and how much they filled my heart with joy. All of it was a gift from you to me.

But Father, in my ignorance I allowed those seasons to define me. I've looked to them for security and meaning instead of looking to you. I've allowed the familiar or the ambitions of my heart to become my salvation. Lord, forgive me. Break this stubbornness off my heart and mind. Resurrect me in Christ to move forward to a new grace for a new day. Give me faith to trust in your love for me.

Hover over my soul and speak light into my darkness. Arrest the fear and confusion that plagues my life and help me walk out each day in the knowledge that although I may not know what the future holds, I can know who holds my future. Lord, I believe. Help me in my unbelief. In Jesus name, Amen.

"The path of the righteous is like the morning sun, shining ever brighter till the full light of day." Proverbs 4:18

Personal Reflection

Read the story of Joseph in Genesis 47-50. Even if you are somewhat familiar with his journey, try to read it in the context of how God works in and through the changing seasons of life.

Try putting yourself in Joseph's place and think on the different fears and terrors he must have prayed through. See if you can discover the season for each purpose and the purpose for each season. And remember, God is the same; yesterday, today, and forever.

_____

_____

_____

_____

_____

_____

_____

_____

_____

_____

_____

_____

_____

_____

_____

FAITH (The Remix)

"Make every effort to add to your faith goodness; and to goodness, knowledge; and to knowledge, self-control; and to self-control, perseverance; and to perseverance, godliness; and to godliness, mutual affection; and to mutual affection, love. For if you possess these qualities in increasing measure, they will keep you from being ineffective and unproductive in your knowledge of our Lord Jesus Christ." 2 Peter1:5-8

Walking out the daily routine with a sensitive ear towards heaven and a willing heart towards prayer can often be one of our greatest expressions of faith. It's not flashy or sexy. It attracts little to no attention. It makes no demands or presumptions. And yet great things can come from simply doing whatever your hands find to do with all your heart as unto the Lord.

Through the daily routine we raise families, develop friendships, start businesses, grow careers, improve communities, overcome obstacles, endure difficulty and strengthen the foundations of the thing God values most; the hearts and souls of people he has preordained us to interact with.

During one of my overly routine days (some folks call them gloomy days), I was lamenting to God about having no one to pray with and talk to. His reply came faster than a speeding bullet. "Why don't you BE someone to pray with," he replied, while simultaneously giving me a vision of exactly what he meant. My reply also came with rapid speed. "You've GOT TO BE KIDDING," I retorted.

A couple hours later I was seated in a lawn chair on the sidewalk along a heavily traveled road a few miles from my home. It was August. Correction, it was mid August in Georgia. For those not familiar with summer in the South, it basically means parking your lawn chair in hell with 150 percent humidity, plus the added bonus of ants, flies, mosquitoes, and zero breeze.

The exact spot where the Lord asked me to sit was directly in front of a Sports Bar, facing the sun with a perfect view of the beautiful shade trees directly across the street. I had two very flimsy homemade poster board signs that read, "If you need prayer, I'm here for you." Each time a car drove past my signs blew over. I spent seven hours swatting bugs, stomping ants, scratching mosquito bits and picking up my pathetic signs. It was a pitiful sight.

No one stopped. Not a single soul the entire day. But I did get a few laughs, honking horns and weird looks. There I was, a college degreed unemployed woman, sitting on the sidewalk in the boiling sun looking like a complete loser. And I felt like a loser. And I told God the same thing in not too pleasant of a manner. Other people were working or networking or enjoying their summer vacation. No one I knew was doing something this insanely ridiculous.

Three o'clock. Four o'clock. Five o'clock. I decided to pack up my circus act and go home. Seven hours completely wasted. All I had to show for it were sweaty clothes, a red face and bug bits. Oh yeah, and wasted money on stupid signs. My next stop, a really good psychiatrist!

While loading my gear in the trunk of my car, I heard a loud voice coming from the door of the Sports Bar. "Wait! Don't leave," the voice shouted. Glancing to my right, I saw a young man in his thirties walking towards the parking lot. Not realizing he was talking to me, I continued loading my car. "Hey! Prayer Chick," he continued. By this time he was standing a few feet away. "You're the Prayer Chick, right?" Shrugging my shoulders I hesitantly replied, "Uh... I... guess?"

Normally I would think it strange for someone to hold their adult beverage between their wrists. But that's exactly what this young man was doing. He didn't do it because he was intoxicated. He held it that way because he had no choice.

"Hello Prayer Chick. My name is Stan." With a beaming smile he continued, "But everyone calls me No Hands Stan." "Don't leave," he demanded. "My friends and I have been watching you all afternoon. Throw your stupid signs in the car and come on in," he demanded. "Everyone's waiting to meet you!"

As I followed no hands Stan in to the bar, God spoke to my heart and said, "This day was all for him. I brought you here for Stan." While God was whispering to me, Stan was yelling to his friends, "Hey guys, this is Prayer Chick." In less than 2 minutes I went from defeated and exhausted, to stunned and surprised.

Almost immediately his friends began to pepper me with countless questions about God and the Bible. Before I could even hoist my buns on the bar stool the questions started flying. It was like a scene from Cheers but with a divine script. "So, Prayer Chick, what does God think about…? Hey Prayer Chick, what does the Bible say about…?" The questions continued for quite a long time.

It was as if they had discovered an alien who could give them first hand information about another planet. They truly wanted answers to issues that had plagued their hearts for years. And they were sincerely interested in my response; everyone except the snarky skeptic at the video poker machine.

Determined not to make eye contact, with an aloof condescension only a crushed embittered heart could exude, he casually commented, "So, how much of a loser do you have to be to sit on a sidewalk in the boiling sun?" Laughing at his question I replied, "I was just praying about that a couple of hours ago. But God showed me that my worth is found in his love for me." Dead silence from the video poker guy. No matter. Stan was the reason I was there.

A few minutes later, and as if on queue, all his friends began to leave. The noise and distractions now subsided I returned my focus on God's divine appointment. "So Stan, what do you do for a living?" I asked. "I run an internet porn site from my house," he answered. Without batting an eye or changing my expression I replied, "So, how's business?" "Truthfully, business is horrible," he explained. "Revenue is down more than seventy percent. I'm about to lose my house and my wife just told me she leaving."

All I could feel was God's love for Stan. It wouldn't have mattered what he said or how he said it. I knew God wanted Stan to experience his love and kindness. It was humbling and exciting just to be a part of that plan. Coincidently, I was also going through similar life challenges and financial reversal. Just like Stan, I too was on the doorstep of bankruptcy. But unlike Stan, I had an assurance of God's love and grace for my life.

A conservative forty something wife and mother was sitting in a local bar sharing the love of God with a porn operator with no hands. It was obvious that God wanted to use our mutual difficulty as a bridge to Stan's heart. So I began to share my life struggles with him. I told him about my hurts and fears, the sleepless nights, the panic attacks and the incredible strain it had put my marriage.

But I also shared how God's love, mercy and grace gave me the strength and faith I needed to walk out each day with hope for the future. "I could really use some of that," Stan replied. He explained that he came to the bar every afternoon to try and overcome the depression. "It's just a temporary relief," he admitted. "I would rather have what you have."

Before I knew it an hour had passed and it was time to go home. Sliding down from the bar stool Stan half heartedly commented, "So, what do you think Prayer Chick? Does God have anything to say to a person like me?" As we walked to the parking lot, I replied. "Stan, God sent me here especially for you. This entire day has been about how much God loves you. None of this was a coincidence. Do you believe it?"

With a quivering lip he answered, "It sure seems that way Prayer Chick. It sure seems that way." Then I asked his permission to pray for him. With tear filled eyes he lowered his head and replied, "Would you? Please."

Participating in a divine set up from heaven is one of the greatest experiences on earth, no matter which side of the event you find yourself on. A divine appointment from God is life changing. It's faith building. It's a hope inspiring. It transforms the ordinary and mundane in to a modern-day miracle.

The Gospels are jammed packed with riveting accounts of miracles and divine encounters that happened in the midst of the mundane. While Christ's followers were working together, walking and talking together, eating together, living and struggling together, he was with them in their daily routine. His voice and presence in the midst of the mundane connected them with the plans and purposes of the Father, and building their faith with each encounter.

That same Jesus has the same desires for us. While we are working together, living together, eating and playing, struggling and stumbling together, Christ wants to engage us in his plans and purposes for our generation. As the Master of our mundane, his hand is constantly directing and redirecting our paths helping us to keep in step with his spirit and building our faith along the way.

I'll bet you've experienced it. I'm sure you've been influenced by his divine direction. It's in our mundane least memorable daily routine that we hear him the most. It may come to us in an unassuming simple idea or thought. Maybe a gentle nudge or shallow whisper saying:

- Let's take a different route to work today.

- Let's pick the kids up 10 minutes early.

- Let's eat somewhere you've never eaten before.

- Let's forget the chores and just spend time together.

- Let's talk with someone who's difficult.

- Let's take a semester off and volunteer with that organization you like.

- Let's stop worrying about the cost and think about the reward.

- Let's focus on the big picture instead of the daily offenses.

- Let's put ourselves in the other person's shoes.

- Let's be someone we would want someone to be for us.

When we know we've heard Gods voice, we can respond because of our faith in the voice we've heard. We go forward in faith because of our experience with the Giver of faith.

In so doing we add to our faith goodness. When we see God's goodness at work we grow in our knowledge of him. The more we know God the more we gain the ability for self-control and the strength to persevere. Godly perseverance makes us more like Christ. That empowers us to grow in mutual affection and love for others. As we desire to hear Gods voice, as we experience him speaking to our hearts, our faith increases. (2 Peter 1:5-8)

And if we are faithful to simply walk out the daily routine with a sensitive ear towards heaven and a willing heart towards prayer we will become more effective in his plans, more engaged in his purposes.

None of us know when our lives will intersect the next miracle moment or divine encounter in the midst of the mundane. Nor should we be preoccupied with trying to make it happen. But we can be proactive by asking God to give us ears to hear, hearts to know and minds to understand. We can also ask him to help us become more sensitive to his voice amongst the noise and busyness of the daily routine. We can ask God to open doors to new experiences that help build our faith.

***

"Be faithful in small things because it is in them that your strength lies."

Mother Teresa of Calcutta

Personal Reflection

_____

_____

_____

_____

_____

_____

_____

_____

_____

_____

_____

_____

_____

_____

_____

_____

_____

_____

_____

_____

_____

_____

MUL-TI-TUDE

Noun – A very great number; the condition or quality of being numerous.

"Above all, love each other deeply, because love covers over a multitude of sins. (I Peter 4:8, New International Version)

"Above all things have intense and unfailing love for one another, for love covers a multitude of sins." (I Peter 4:8, Amplified Bible)

"Above all, keep fervent in your love for one another, because love covers a multitude of sins." (I Peter 4:8, New American Standard Bible)

"Most important of all, continue to show deep love for each other, for love covers a multitude of sins." (I Peter 4:8, New Living Translation)

Above all, keep loving one another ear-
nestly, since love covers a multitude of sins.
(I Peter 4:8, English Standard Version)

Before he met Jesus, Peter was a hard working entrepreneur, struggling to earn a living in an unpredictable line of work. Like any business person worth their salt, he understood the importance of managing risk. The fishing business was unforgiving. The never ending demand to balance investments and expenses taught him to calculate life from the perspective of risk and reward. But Peter was also a Jew raised in the Hebrew traditions and the Law of Moses. So when he inquired of Jesus about forgiveness, those two paradigms greatly influenced his ideas on the subject.

Matthew 18:21 records his question. "Then Peter came up and said to him, Lord, how often will my brother sin against me, and I forgive him, as many as seven times?" At that point in his life, he didn't view forgiveness as a gift or a worthwhile investment. At that point in his life forgiveness was just plain costly, and a cost he judged was all on him. In spite of what the scriptures had instructed, forgiving the same person seven times was more than reasonable, and probably six times too many for his risk tolerance. Ironically, Peter made no inquiry as to how many times some one else should forgive him.

But a strange thing happened on the way to 1Peter 4:8 that transformed his understanding. The rough and tough calculating seaman was hand-picked by Forgiveness itself and called to "Go Fishing" for the very people who caused him so much grief. During those life altering years, he observed how Jesus never separated himself from the inconveniences, selfishness, and presumption of those around him. He saw how Jesus was never disappointed by events or surprised by peoples' choices.

In fact, Jesus was probably the first person Peter ever knew who didn't worry about how another persons' behavior might impact his life or how their decisions would affect his future, his livelihood, his influence, or his reputation. For more than 1,000 days, Peter lived with someone who showed sacrificial love and forgiveness to all without seeking an ounce of anything in return. He also saw how Jesus responded to a multitude of betrayal, a multitude of insult, a multitude of mistreatment, abandonment, and then finally a violent agonizing death. Peter watched a blameless innocent man respond to all of those events with zero retaliation or bitterness, and zero demand for justice or sympathy.

I'm sure the hot tempered do-it-yourselfer often wondered how Jesus did all of those things without losing his sanity? Maybe it was because Jesus knew who he was and he knew who's he was. He knew he had come from the Father and that he would return to the Father (John 13:3). In other words, he knew his past and his future were secure. But Jesus also had first-hand experience with the Father's resources and experienced every need of His life being met to the fullest. And since He lived everyday with no unmet need (wow, what a concept), He simply gave the overflow of the Fathers resources to those around Him.

In time, Peter became the recipient of that same love, on more than one occasion. He experienced being forgiven for a multitude of denial, a multitude of unbelief, a multitude of impatience, and a multitude of short sightedness. Because of God's love and forgiveness, Peter received a multitude of restoration and a multitude of hope, direction and purpose. He experienced being covered by Love, and it changed his perspective about loving and covering others.

Now before you get too excited about loving the unlovable, turning the other cheek, or bearing with someone's unbearable personality, let me remind you that God does not expect us to do any of it in our own strength. Just like everything else in Christianity, the ability to love and cover a multitude of offense is a God created ability. It comes from experiencing God's resources of forgiveness for our sins. It comes from knowing the gift of grace to perfectly meet the needs of our life. That's what Peter came to understand.

So with that perspective as our backdrop, let's take a look at some possible fishing expeditions God might be calling us to. Let's discover how we can journey towards 1 Peter 4:8 concerning the multitude of challenges life sends our way.

When you get a call from the county jail asking you to post bail for the third time in six months, remember that Love covers a multitude of irresponsibility.

I'm not suggesting that you bail them out. Just be willing to pray about how the person and the situation provoke you. Be honest with God about it. Do you want to write them off? Are you tempted to judge them as a loser who will never get their act together? Maybe that's how they feel about their life and situation. Maybe some past event or experience caused them to make a debilitating judgment about their life and their future.

It's possible their behavior is simply an outward expression of a judgment they made. That might explain (not excuse) their behavior. Put yourself in their shoes the way Jesus did for us. Or maybe Take an Eye Exam. Have you ever felt hopeless? Ever felt like a failure? Ever felt like the deck was stacked against you? Why did you feel those feelings? Was it because you saw no way out, no solution, no one to turn to, not even God? Perhaps that's what controls them as well.

Then pray for them the same way you would want someone to pray for you. Ask God to intervene in their life and be their way of escape the way he has for you. Ask Him to forgive them for looking to the bottle, the pill, or the wrong crowd for help. And ask God to forgive your unbelief in His ability to show up on that persons' behalf. Maybe they feel the same way. Think about it…just think about it.

When you've given your all to a relationship, sacrificed your time for the other person, worked hard to resolve differences yet none of it is reciprocated, remember that Love covers a multitude of self centeredness.

I know you're ready to close the door on this relationship. Maybe you're exhausted with frustration and anger. Maybe you don't see any possible way things will ever change. But would you please take a minute and consider a few Divine Questions. Can you love this person even if there is nothing in it for you? Can you hang in there even if they never meet a single need of your heart? Can you sacrifice for someone who might never sacrifice for you? Probably not. But that's okay. Remember being honest is a great place to start.

The truth is, none of us can do this unless God creates it in us and unless we experience our needs being fully met by God. When that happens we are free to simply love others with the love God has created in us. Think about it like this. God loves us with a love no one could ever match. His love is the most complete love we could ever know and He created us for that purpose. Now, do you think He would want us to spend our life trying to get our needs met from someone who can't meet them?

The other person is just as needy for God's love to complete their life (although they may not realize it). So what if both of you could finally find your fulfillment in God? Then you could simply enjoy each other without placing supernatural demands on mere flesh and blood. Don't have that? Then Think Loaves and Fishes. Just give Jesus one piece of your heart concerning this issue. In other words, don't get overwhelmed thinking that you have to boil the ocean. Just be willing to pray about the little things, a little piece at a time. Ask God to give you a new frame of reference and a new experience of Him meeting the need in both your hearts. Instead of focusing on what your not getting from the relationship, think about what your need from God concerning all your relationships. You can let it drive you crazy or you can let it drive you to the cross. The choice is yours.

When you're banging your head in frustration because the other person refuses to see how their thinking is going to send them over a cliff and you're on the verge of giving them their wish, remember that Love covers a multitude of immaturity.

Have you ever been naive? Remember when your cavalier attitude convinced you of your own immortality? Remember pledging your devotion to a panacea and placing all your faith in it?

Here's a Divine Question to ponder: If they could just see things your way how would it make you feel? Would it give you a sense of peace or rest for your soul? I'll bet they're convinced their decisions will give them the same thing. Then try taking an Eye Exam. Afterwards notice if your heart changes from judgment and fault finding to love and understanding. It's the "Love of God" not the law of religion or societal expectations that brings a soul to their senses. Still don't believe me? Then think about this question; Has your approach produced good fruit the way the Bible

150

describes it; (love, joy, peace, patience, gentleness, kindness, self control)? Repeat after me; Love is patient and kind... it does not demand its own way. (1 Corinthians 13:4-5). ☺

When you're tired of footing the bill for others who find it easier to make excuses than to take responsibility, remember that Love covers a multitude of entitlement.

People with an entitlement mentality can be reluctant to change because they feel entitled to be entitled and don't understand why you have a problem with it. But in our effort to demand their change, we demonstrate a different kind of entitlement. Let me explain.

Their demand is to have their way. Our demand is that they stop demanding their way. They demand we pay the cost. We demand they pay the cost. They demand we understand. We demand they grow up and take responsibility. Their peace comes from depending on others. Our peace comes from depending on our self.

They can't believe God will be there for them so they look to others as a substitute. We can't believe God will be there for us so we look to ourselves which makes them just one more burden that distracts us. One side looks weak the other looks strong, but both fall short of the love and grace of God.

I think it's safe to say this type of endless head butting has kept a lot of radio and television commentators very wealthy. It's also kept a large number of politicians permanently employed. It divides families, friends, neighbors, churches, colleagues, etc. And it is seldom resolved through intellectual reasoning or debate because each side is convinced of their own rightness. So where does it end? At the Cross of course. The problem is, someone has to go first.

I know that smacks and is almost as offensive as the person who is driving you crazy. However, it is in moments like this when we can appreciate the sacrifice Jesus made for us. Remember what he told the disciples, "As the Father sent me, so I send you." Well… the Father sent him to die for us. Jesus went first on our behalf because someone had to. Otherwise we would never experience reconciliation with the Father or deliverance from the slime that was destroying us?

Most of the time we think our version of right and wrong is the standard everyone else should live by. But remember, unless your standard is the person of Jesus, it's just another standard. Human standards always fall short of the love and grace of God.

Peace of mind is what we need most. Peace that passes all understanding, peace that surpasses the effect of entitlement. If you can know God's love and grace being greater than the demands others place on you, then you will be able to forgive them, your heart can find rest and your prayers will open the door for the Holy Spirit to convict and change them. Resign from trying to reason with them. Only God can do that in such a way that brings about repentance. Our job is to forgive. His job is to convict of sin.

***

In the year leading up to my father's death, he was in an out of intensive care numerous times. When he was admitted two days after Christmas the doctors pronounced a diagnosis none of us were prepared to hear. "Mr. Lowery," they explained, "your heart is no longer working. There is nothing else we can do to help you."

What do you talk about when your loved one is only hours from leaving this world? More importantly, what parting words does the person who's leaving give those who are left behind? The finality of the doctor's prognosis brought another finality to my mind. The words I longed to hear from my dad would never be said. And it ripped my heart to pieces. Was he really going to die and never say what I had always wanted to hear? It was so gut wrenching, I cried out to God in prayer. This was my conversation.

Me: Lord, my dad is dying and I will never hear him say that he is proud of me. I'll never hear him tell me I was a good daughter, a good wife and mother, or that he is proud of my accomplishments. I'm never going to hear any of it! Not ever.

God: What is it you really want to hear from your dad? What do you want to hear him say the most?

Me: … (deep sigh) I want him to hold my hand, look me in the eyes and say "Well done daughter. Well done." That's what I want to hear.

God: Sweetheart, you're never going to hear those words from your dad… but you WILL hear them from me! You will defiantly hear those words from me!

Immediately my tears of agony flowed in to tears of joy and peace. Although I would never hear those faithful words from my earthly father, the assurance of hearing them from my Heavenly Father transformed my heart. It healed the wounds I feared would stay with me a lifetime. God also showed me that my dad had never heard those faithful words for himself. He was on his death bed and had yet to hear "Well Done" from anyone. That revelation changed my entire perspective.

The next evening, the Lord gave me a divine open door to spend quality time with my dad. I decided to use it as an opportunity to once again, express my gratitude to him for all he had taught me and all the things he had done to help me navigate through life. He was conscious though unable to speak. But I could tell he was enjoying our conversation about old times and crazy stories that ushered in the enduring life lessons I will always be grateful for. As I stood at his bedside, all I could feel was God's love for both of us. In spite of a lifelong strained relationship, the only thing that mattered was what mattered most to God.

For the first time ever there was no tension or distance between us, only the love and grace of God for a daughter and her dad. Gazing in to his blue eyes now weak and frail I squeezed his hand a little tighter. Leaning in closer I tenderly whispered, "The main thing I came to tell you is… Well done Daddy. WELL DONE!" As if resting from a long and tiring journey, his entire body surrendered to a place of deep relaxation and peace. Then looking toward the window and the moon lit sky, he gently closed his eyes and drifted off to sleep. That was the last conversation I had with my dad. "Well done" were the last words he heard me say. A few hours later my father was gone.

All my life I had assumed my dad was capable of giving me what I longed for. The years of waiting and not receiving felt like a multitude of rejection, a multitude of insensitivity, a multitude of missed opportunity, a multitude of love withheld. The truth is he simply did not have it to give because he had never received it for himself. But the whole truth is only my Heavenly Father could say what I needed to hear in a way that would satisfy my soul. Only God could meet the needs of my heart to such a degree that I could give the overflow to someone else.

What I'm trying to say is that once we experience the love of God for our hurts and disappointments, when we receive from Jesus what we are seeking from people, we can more easily forgive and then give back. More importantly, we can know the Father the same way Jesus does. We can have the original God connection Adam and Eve had before The Fall.

The Bible says that perfect love cast out all fear. That includes the fear of loss, the fear of neglect, the fear of failure, the fear of tomorrow, the fear of our own shortcomings and the fear of other people's mistakes. The degree to which we take hold of the perfect love of God through the person of Jesus Christ, is the same degree to which we experience freedom from fear; for ourselves, for others and for our circumstances.

Only a God created love can cover a multitude of sin. Only his Spirit at work in us can heal the cumulative effect of offenses we experience in this life. Only God's love can meet the needs of our heart and soul. So even if the other person never changes, what's the downside in finding the perfect love of God for you? Even if they continue to act selfish or pig headed, what's the downside in finding all your needs met in Christ? Even if the other person never meets a single need of your heart, what's the downside in finding the peace that passes all understanding? What's the downside in discovering Love that covers a multitude of sins?

Heavenly Father,

I really don't have love that covers a multitude of sin. And yet your love is always there to cover me and I thank you for that. I know you don't condemn me because I know you want to transform me to be more like you. I guess I just never realized how badly I needed your help in this matter.

Father, the truth I find it difficult to cover the faults of others because I'm fearful of what their behavior will cost me. Rather than trusting you to make up the difference I cover up my fear with fault finding, nit picking or demands for the other person to change. Lord, forgive me and give me the ability to be patient with others the way you have been patient with me. Help me to cover and love others the way you have loved and covered me.

Help me to see just how much you have forgiven my weakness and shortcomings so that I can more easily forgive the weakness and shortcomings of others. Quench my demand for restoration and justice from others by giving me a greater sense of your sovereignty, grace and mercy at work in my life.

Help me to rest in the eternal truth that in all things you are truly at work for my good. Empower me, by your Holy Spirit, to draw upon your endless reservoir of love for me so I might give the overflow to others. Amen.

***

"Most of all, love each other as if your life depended on it. Love makes up for practically anything." (I Peter 4:8, The Message Bible)

Personal Reflection

_____

_____

_____

_____

_____

_____

_____

_____

_____

_____

_____

_____

_____

_____

_____

_____

_____

_____

_____

INVITE-U

My dad waited 78 years to hear someone say, "Well done." But you don't have to. If you are a child of God, if you have made Jesus your Savior, then rest assured these beautiful words await you as the Last Will and Testament over your life. It's a guarantee! I pray the realization of this will permeate your heart and mind. I pray it brings complete acceptance and validation as it did to me. So whether you were a believer in Jesus Christ before reading this book, or you made a decision along the way, please rest in the knowledge that your Heavenly Father has a bright and promising future custom made just for you. He loves you. He cares for you. He has predestined you to know him and grow in the knowledge of his love for you.

If, on the other hand, there is uncertainty about your connection to God, you can reconcile all that today. You can know without a doubt that your mistakes are covered. You can know for certain your shortcomings are redeemed. You can know the peace that comes from complete forgiveness of sin. You too can have the guarantee of hearing, "Well done good and faithful servant. Enter into your Father's rest." Can you feel the loving tug of God's spirit on your heart right now? I can feel it.

That tugging is a custom designed invitation to a custom designed child of the Creator. He is calling you to your bright and beautiful future. So let's go there together. Haven't you waited long enough? Let's pray this life changing prayer and usher in the changed life you've been longing for.

"Heavenly Father, I tried to make the best of what life has given me. Even though I thought I was doing the right thing in each situation, I realize that turning to myself or the world was the opposite of what I truly needed. I now know I should have turned to you. Thank you for being so faithful to bring me to this pivotal moment in time. Thank you for ordaining all my steps so that I can step in to a new life as your child. Forgive me for all the ways I have tried to provide for my own salvation. Forgive my ignorance, forgive my stubbornness and forgive my complacency. Most of all forgive my sins. I am truly sorry for all the ways I misjudged you or misunderstood who you are and the value you place on my life. I asked that the mountain of experience that has hindered me from knowing you would be crucified on the Cross. Lord Jesus, resurrect me with a new operating system in my soul and spirit, in my heart and mind. Lead me and guide me to a greater sense of connection with you unlike anything I have ever known. And because I know that I am incapable of bringing any of this to pass in my own strength, I ask for your mercy and peace for the journey ahead. Seal my heart with your Holy Spirit from this day forward. In Jesus name Amen.

If you prayed this prayer to receive Jesus as your Lord and Savior, then let me be the first to say... WELCOME TO THE FAMILY OF GOD! Secondly, please email me and tell me about your experience. You can also send your prayer request or questions you might have to my website or email. I want to hear from you. God bless you and lets stay in touch!

TawanaLowery@hotmail.com
www.prayereagles.com

Personal Reflection

SECTION THREE

HOW TO PRAY THE SCRIPTURES

In my own life, the scriptures have served as the cornerstone of productive effectual prayer. God's Word has helped to bring healing, encouragement, wisdom, perseverance and faith to my daily living. When a particular passage speaks to me regarding an idea or situation, I write it down on an index card. Sometimes I write the date on the back and a short sentence about how that scripture inspired me to pray.

Reading a scripture then writing it down then reading it again as a prayer feeds the mind with divine truth. I consider it my spiritual contingency planning. Some of my prayer cards date back more than 15 years. And they still hold great relevancy today. That's what I love most about God's Word. The Bible says that "the Word of the Lord endures forever." Something lasting. Something dependable. Something that never changes. That sound good to me!

If you've never practiced this technique, I challenge you to start today. The Scriptures not only guide our prayers, they provide instructions for life and offer insight to the personhood of God himself.

The Psalms are a great place to begin. Consider reading one each day. Jot down specific verses that speak to you. Then read them as a prayer.

Another good place to start is with the book of Proverbs. Coincidently, there are 31 chapters in Proverbs. That's one chapter for each day of the month. One technique would be to read the same Proverb twice each day. Read it in the morning then again before bed. Proverbs is also known as the book of wisdom. Who doesn't need a steady diet of that?

The following scriptures are a few of my absolute favorites. I've included examples of how to make the passage personal so it can be incorporated in to your prayers as well. Feel free to use my list as a starting place to build your own.

MY SCRIPTURE FAVS

John 1:17

*From the fullness of his grace, we receive
one blessing after another.*

Making it a personal: "Lord I thank you that from the endless abundance of your grace I am blessed over and over and over again. Forgive me for looking to my resources for blessing. All blessing comes from you alone."

Romans 8:28

*And we know that in all things God works
for the good of all those who love him and
have been called according to his purpose.*

Making it personal: "Regardless of what is happening in my life right now, God is at work for my good. No matter the circumstance or challenge, my Father is actively at work on my behalf, using it all for a future greater than I can imagine.

2 Peter 1:3

*His divine power has given us everything
we need for life and godliness through
our knowledge of him who called us by his
own glory and goodness.*

2 Corinthians 9:8

*And God is able to make all grace abound
to you, so that in all things at all times having all that you need you will abound in
every good work.*

Making it personal: Today, right now at this very moment, God grace is abundant towards me. Whatever is taking place in my life, wherever the day may take me, I can rest in God's grace. In him and through him I have all that I need."

Psalm 84:11-12

The Lord bestows favor and honor; no good thing does he withhold from those whose walk is blameless. Blessed is the man who trusts in the Lord.

Making it personal: "The Lord covers me with his favor and honor. Every good thing I need he will supply it. As my trust in him increases, his blessings will increase in my life."

Psalm 5:12

For surely, O Lord, you bless the righteous; you surround them with favor as with a shield.

Making it personal: "The Lord himself, surrounds me with favor on every side. And nothing can stop his blessings towards me."

Philippians 2:14

Do everything without complaining or arguing so that you may become blameless and pure, a child of God without fault in a crooked and depraved generation.

Deuteronomy 8:18

Remember the Lord your God, for it is he who gives you the ability to produce wealth and so confirms his covenant.

Making it personal: Father I thank you for giving me the ability to work and produce wealth. Thank you for ideas, for strength and courage. When I am tempted with despair, remind me of this truth. Give me the strength I need to keep going forward as I put more and more faith in you."

Ephesians 3:20

God is able to do immeasurably more than all I think or even imagine according to his power at work in me.

Making it personal: "Lord forgive me for putting my life in a box of my own limitations and experiences. Help me to trust in your unlimited unsearchable goodness towards me."

I Chronicles 29:11-12

Everything in the heavens and the earth is yours, Oh Lord, and this is your kingdom. We adore you for being in control of everything. Riches and honor come from you alone and you are the ruler of all mankind. Your hand controls power and might, and it is at your discretion that men are made great and given strength.

Romans 12:12

Be joyful is hope, patient in affliction, faithful in prayer.

Making it personal: Father I am struck with just how impossible it is to do any of this apart from you. Give me grace to be joyful when hope is prolonged. Give me supernatural patience when affliction visits my life. And most of all Father, I ask for faith to continue reaching out to you even when I want to give up."

I Thessalonians 5:16-18

Be joyful always, pray continually, give thanks in all circumstances, for this is the will of God for you in Christ Jesus.

Matthew 7:12

So in everything, do unto others as you would have them do unto you, for this sums up the law and the prophets.

Psalm 112:4

Even in darkness light dawns for the upright, for the gracious and compassionate person.

Making it personal: "No matter how dark and uncertain life seems right now the Lord is fashioning a bright future for me. His light is always dawning in my life today."

Jeremiah 29:11

For I know the plans I have for you, says the Lord. Plans to prosper you and not to harm you, plans to give you a hope and a future.

Making it personal: "The Lords plans for ME are to prosper me and not to harm me. Because he loves me, I have hope. No matter what the circumstance, God has a bright future in store for me."

Most Frequently Read Bible Verses

John 3:16

"For God so loved the world that he gave his one and only Son, that whoever believes in him shall not perish but have eternal life.

Isaiah 41:10

So do not fear, for I am with you; do not be dismayed, for I am your God. I will strengthen you and help you; I will uphold you with my righteous right hand.

Psalm 23:1-6

The LORD is my shepherd, I shall not be in want. He makes me lie down in green pastures, he leads me beside quiet waters, he restores my soul. He guides me in paths of righteousness for his name's sake. Even though I walk through the valley of the shadow of death, I will fear no evil, for you are with me; your rod and your staff, they comfort me. You prepare a table before me in the presence of my enemies. You anoint my head with oil; my cup overflows. Surely goodness and love will follow me all the days of my life, and I will dwell in the house of the LORD forever.

Proverbs 3:5-6

Trust in the LORD with all your heart and lean not on your own understanding; in all your ways acknowledge him, and he will make your paths straight.

Galatians 5:22-23

But the fruit of the Spirit is love, joy, peace, patience, kindness, goodness, faithfulness, gentleness and self-control. Against such things there is no law.

2 Corinthians 5:17

Therefore, if anyone is in Christ, he is a new creation; the old has gone, the new has come!

James 5:16

Therefore confess your sins to each other and pray for each other so that you may be healed. The prayer of a righteous man is powerful and effective.

Deuteronomy 31:6

Be strong and courageous. Do not be afraid or terrified because of them, for the LORD your God goes with you; he will never leave you nor forsake you."

Jeremiah 29:11

For I know the plans I have for you," declares the LORD, "plans to prosper you and not to harm you, plans to give you hope and a future.

1 Corinthians 13:4-8

Love is patient, love is kind. It does not envy, it does not boast, it is not proud. It is not rude, it is not self-seeking, it is not easily angered, it keeps no record of wrongs. Love does not delight in evil but rejoices with the truth. It always protects, always trusts, always hopes, always perseveres. Love never fails. But where there are prophecies, they will cease; where there are tongues, they will be stilled; where there is knowledge, it will pass away.

Philippians 4:13

I can do everything through him who gives me strength.

Romans 8:28

And we know that in all things God works for the good of those who love him, who have been called according to his purpose.

Hebrews 11:1

Now faith is being sure of what we hope for and certain of what we do not see.

2 Timothy 1:7

For God did not give us a spirit of timidity, but a spirit of power, of love and of self-discipline.

1 Corinthians 10:13

No temptation has seized you except what is common to man. And God is faithful; he will not let you be tempted beyond what you can bear. But when you are tempted, he will also provide a way out so that you can stand up under it.

Isaiah 40:31

But those who hope in the LORD will renew their strength. They will soar on wings like eagles; they will run and not grow weary, they will walk and not be faint.

Joshua 1:9

Have I not commanded you? Be strong and courageous. Do not be terrified; do not be discouraged, for the LORD your God will be with you wherever you go."

Philippians 4:6

Do not be anxious about anything, but in everything, by prayer and petition, with thanksgiving, present your requests to God.

John 10:10

The thief comes only to steal and kill and destroy; I have come that they may have life, and have it to the full.

Zephaniah 3:17

The LORD your God is with you, he is mighty to save. He will take great delight

in you, he will quiet you with his love, he
will rejoice over you with singing."

Matthew 11:28

"Come to me, all you who are weary and
burdened, and I will give you rest.

You can also search the web for specific Bible verses on topics you might be interested in, such as encouragement, fear, depression, addiction, faith, peace and so on. A couple of internet sites I like to reference are:

* www.openbible.info/topics/

* www.biblestudytools.com/topical-verses/

The important thing is to be proactive and intentional about filling your mind with God's Word. Consider it your spiritual exercise plan.

I want to share these final two scriptures as my prayer for you.

Psalm 37:23-24

The Lord directs the steps of the godly.
He delights in every detail of their lives.
Though they stumble they will never fall
for the Lord holds them by the hand.

My personal prayer for you:

"Heavenly Father, I ask that you would inten-sionally direct this dear ones steps. In fact Lord, I pray that they will come to the understanding of exactly how much joy you take in every de-tail of their life. I pray that even when they are stumbling or bumbling, I ask they will rest in the truth that you will never let them fall. Give them a greater sense of you holding them by the hand and that nothing will ever cause you to let them go. Amen"

And finally...

I pray the Lord bless you and keep you. I asked that the Lord make His face to shine upon you, and be gracious to you. May the Lord turn his face toward you and give you peace now and forever more. (Num-bers 6:24-26)

LET ME HEAR FROM YOU!

If this book has been meaningful to you, or if you prayed to accept Christ as your Savior, I would love to hear from you. You can email me at TawanaLowery@hotmail.com. Feel free to tell me your story or send me any prayer request you might have. If you would like to host a prayer seminar or prayer training for your team, please write to me about your organization and what you would like to accomplish. God bless you.

Made in the USA
Columbia, SC
20 February 2023